I0012111

Learning AngularJS Animations

Enhance user experience with awesome animations in AngularJS using CSS and JavaScript

Richard Keller

BIRMINGHAM - MUMBAI

Learning AngularJS Animations

Copyright © 2014 Packt Publishing

All rights reserved. No part of this book may be reproduced, stored in a retrieval system, or transmitted in any form or by any means, without the prior written permission of the publisher, except in the case of brief quotations embedded in critical articles or reviews.

Every effort has been made in the preparation of this book to ensure the accuracy of the information presented. However, the information contained in this book is sold without warranty, either express or implied. Neither the author, nor Packt Publishing, and its dealers and distributors will be held liable for any damages caused or alleged to be caused directly or indirectly by this book.

Packt Publishing has endeavored to provide trademark information about all of the companies and products mentioned in this book by the appropriate use of capitals. However, Packt Publishing cannot guarantee the accuracy of this information.

First published: October 2014

Production reference: 1251014

Published by Packt Publishing Ltd.
Livery Place
35 Livery Street
Birmingham B3 2PB, UK.

ISBN 978-1-78398-442-8

www.packtpub.com

Credits

Author

Richard Keller

Reviewers

Douglas Duteil

Amit Gharat

Daniel Mackay

Sathish VJ

Commissioning Editor

Pramila Balan

Acquisition Editor

Greg Wild

Content Development Editor

Rohit Kumar Singh

Technical Editors

Mrunmayee Patil

Shruti Rawool

Copy Editors

Deepa Nambiar

Stuti Srivastava

Project Coordinator

Mary Alex

Proofreaders

Simran Bhogal

Ameesha Green

Paul Hindle

Clyde Jenkins

Indexer

Rekha Nair

Production Coordinator

Arvindkumar Gupta

Cover Work

Arvindkumar Gupta

About the Author

Richard Keller obtained his BSc in Computer Science from State University of Campinas (UNICAMP), Brazil. He is currently a software engineer at Spring Mobile Solutions in the Latin America headquarters located in São Paulo. His work there includes analysis and implementation of systems used by customer's headquarters and development of internal tools to enhance the company's productivity. He works with the AngularJS framework on a daily basis and with a variety of other technologies including TypeScript, C#, and SQL Server.

He previously worked for an online marketplace for handmade items, a mobile payment company, and an open source e-learning project in an institute at UNICAMP.

I would like to thank my parents and family for all their support for my education and personal growth. In addition, I would like to thank the open source community of AngularJS and the AngularJS core team for developing and improving this great framework every day. Finally, I am thankful to my girlfriend for supporting me while writing this book.

About the Reviewers

Douglas Duteil is a young open source contributor and a part of the Directory team of the Angular UI organization since 2012. He's passionate about web user interfaces, web user experience, and web components.

While pursuing his Master's degree in Computer Science at University of Paris 8, Douglas had the opportunity to work on digital literature with a group of artists such as Kalamar-e Kidz and the New Fire Tree Press.

He's now working with SFEIR, Paris, a software development company, and participates in the ngParis meetup.

Amit Gharat is a full stack engineer, open source contributor, and co-author for *AngularJS UI Development*, *Packt Publishing*. He has built and made some of his personal projects open source, such as Directives, SPAs, and Chrome Extensions written in AngularJS. He has an urge to share his programming experiences in an easy-to-understand language through his personal blog (`http://amitgharat.wordpress.com`) in order to inspire and help others. When not programming, Amit enjoys reading and watching YouTube and comedy shows with his family.

I would like to thank my family who has encouraged me to do so.

Daniel Mackay has 9 years of commercial experience, primarily in the Microsoft stack, and is currently a lead developer at a software consultancy in Sydney, Australia.

He is passionate about all things in web and particularly enjoys working with ASP.NET MVC, Web API, and Entity Framework. He considers himself a very well-rounded developer and is not afraid to get thrown into the deep end of frontend development. Over the past few years, he has been concentrating on full-stack web development, including technologies such as HTML5, JavaScript, and CSS3. He has built a large commercial single-page application with AngularJS, which is used by a major telecommunications company in Australia. He is a big believer of process and is always searching for the most productive tool for the job.

He is very passionate about technology and is continually improving himself whenever possible through conferences, blogs, books, and personal projects.

When not coding, you'll probably find him halfway up a cliff in the Blue Mountains, or catching a wave at one of Sydney's many beautiful beaches.

Sathish VJ is a technologist who is passionate about software specifically — where he is most prolific — and all science, engineering, and technology in general. He regularly attends hackathons, quickly prototyping new ideas on various emerging technologies. He has always been particularly interested in AngularJS, conducting many workshops and training events for the community and has created almost all his recent apps in AngularJS.

www.PacktPub.com

Support files, eBooks, discount offers, and more

You might want to visit www.PacktPub.com for support files and downloads related to your book.

Did you know that Packt offers eBook versions of every book published, with PDF and ePub files available? You can upgrade to the eBook version at www.PacktPub.com and as a print book customer, you are entitled to a discount on the eBook copy. Get in touch with us at service@packtpub.com for more details.

At www.PacktPub.com, you can also read a collection of free technical articles, sign up for a range of free newsletters and receive exclusive discounts and offers on Packt books and eBooks.

http://PacktLib.PacktPub.com

Do you need instant solutions to your IT questions? PacktLib is Packt's online digital book library. Here, you can access, read and search across Packt's entire library of books.

Why subscribe?

- Fully searchable across every book published by Packt
- Copy and paste, print and bookmark content
- On demand and accessible via web browser

Free access for Packt account holders

If you have an account with Packt at www.PacktPub.com, you can use this to access PacktLib today and view nine entirely free books. Simply use your login credentials for immediate access.

Table of Contents

Preface

The AngularJS framework is a turning point in the evolution of web development. It really helps developers to produce professional web apps by writing less JavaScript code.

The ngAnimate module, developed by the core team of AngularJS and the open source community, integrated AngularJS features with animation web standards, providing all the benefits from standardization with AngularJS development patterns.

Before animations were introduced to AngularJS, integrating animations was a bit tricky, as in AngularJS, changes to the model affect the view implicitly (it's part of the two-way data binding concept). In other words, the DOM life cycle management is often controlled by the AngularJS core and animations should be triggered in between those manipulations. To solve this problem, the ngAnimate module was written and redesigned to be completely based on CSS classes. This means that animations should be applied based on element classes. Classes are appended or removed from elements on specific events, so we are able to apply animations as the entry of an element on DOM and the imminent exit of an element from DOM.

This book will help you learn from the beginning how to add animations to AngularJS web apps, focusing on the ngAnimate module. It's an optional module in AngularJS because the framework is going in a direction that will allow you to choose which modules to use so that the module can fit your needs and be as light as you desire.

What this book covers

Chapter 1, Getting Started, will introduce you to the history of animations in web development and explain why the AngularJS animation module is so important. Then, you will get started on the modern web standards of animation, introducing you to when to use each of them.

Chapter 2, Understanding CSS3 Transitions and Animations, will teach you how to create animations using CSS transitions, CSS animations, and how to animate using the CSS transform, giving us a good base to start using animations with the AngularJS framework in the next chapter.

Chapter 3, Creating Our First Animation in AngularJS, will walk you through setting up an AngularJS application using the ngAnimate module. Then, we will create basic animations using CSS transitions and an animation keyframe integrated with AngularJS native directives. This chapter will introduce the AngularJS directives that support animation events.

Chapter 4, JavaScript Animations in AngularJS, will tell you how to create animations using JavaScript and create animations with jQuery integrated with AngularJS native directives. You will learn how to create animations using CSS and JavaScript as a fallback when the browser does not support CSS animations.

Chapter 5, Custom Directives and the $animate Service, will teach you how to use CSS animations together with custom directives by giving you an overview of what happens in the life cycle of an AngularJS animation inside the $animate service. Then, it will teach you how to create animations in custom directives using only JavaScript.

Chapter 6, Animations for Mobile Devices, will help you apply animations to enhance usability on smartphones and small devices and introduces the Google material design, a guideline for mobile development.

Chapter 7, Staggering Animations, will teach you how to create animations that appear in a consistent sequence, which are usually difficult to create without the ngAnimate module, and can improve user experience. This chapter will teach you the rules to be followed and how to apply these animations in native and custom directives.

Chapter 8, Animations Performance Optimization, will provide you with an introduction to animation performance diagnostics and solutions by teaching you how to find performance bottlenecks using Chrome DevTools. Then, it will teach you about rendering layers and animations that you should avoid or are that replaced by others.

What you need for this book

In order to run the example code in this book, you will need a modern web browser such as Google Chrome, IE10 or newer, Safari, or Firefox, as support for CSS animations and CSS transitions is mandatory.

A basic text editor is mandatory to test samples and answer exercises.

Source files of AngularJS and angular animate are needed too, although we will use a CDN for all samples.

Who this book is for

This book is intended for those who are familiar with the AngularJS framework, as we will focus on the animations module. You need to know the basics of HTML and CSS. Some previous knowledge about the most essential AngularJS directives (such as ngRepeat, ngView, ngIf, and ngSwitch) is expected, but no previous knowledge of JavaScript animations, CSS3 animations, or any animations library is required.

By reading this book, you will be prepared to create animations and integrate them with AngularJS web apps.

Conventions

In this book, you will find a number of styles of text that distinguish between different kinds of information. Here are some examples of these styles and an explanation of their meaning.

Code words in text, database table names, folder names, filenames, file extensions, pathnames, dummy URLs, user input, and Twitter handles are shown as follows: "First we created an animation with JavaScript without `requestFrameRate`."

A block of code is set as follows:

```
var app = angular.module('myApp', ['ngAnimate'])
    .animation(".firstJsAnimation", firstJsAnimation);
```

When we wish to draw your attention to a particular part of a code block, the relevant lines or items are set in bold:

```
<body>
  <script src="//ajax.googleapis.com/ajax/libs/angularjs/
    1.3.0/angular.min.js"></script>
  <script src="//ajax.googleapis.com/ajax/libs/angularjs/
    1.3.0/angular-animate.min.js"></script>
  <script>
    var app = angular.module('myApp', ['ngAnimate']);
  </script>
</body>
```

New terms and **important words** are shown in bold. Words that you see on the screen, in menus or dialog boxes for example, appear in the text like this: "For this sample, we have a **Toggle fade** button that changes the ngShow model value, so we can see what happens when the element fades in and fades out from the DOM."

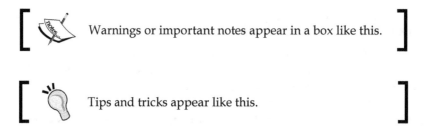

> Warnings or important notes appear in a box like this.

> Tips and tricks appear like this.

Reader feedback

Feedback from our readers is always welcome. Let us know what you think about this book—what you liked or may have disliked. Reader feedback is important for us to develop titles that you really get the most out of.

To send us general feedback, simply send an e-mail to feedback@packtpub.com, and mention the book title via the subject of your message.

If there is a topic that you have expertise in and you are interested in either writing or contributing to a book, see our author guide on www.packtpub.com/authors.

Customer support

Now that you are the proud owner of a Packt book, we have a number of things to help you to get the most from your purchase.

Downloading the example code

You can download the example code files for all Packt books you have purchased from your account at http://www.packtpub.com. If you purchased this book elsewhere, you can visit http://www.packtpub.com/support and register to have the files e-mailed directly to you.

Downloading the color images of this book

We also provide you a PDF file that has color images of the screenshots/diagrams used in this book. The color images will help you better understand the changes in the output. You can download this file from: `https://www.packtpub.com/sites/default/files/downloads/4428OS_ColoredImages.pdf`.

Errata

Although we have taken every care to ensure the accuracy of our content, mistakes do happen. If you find a mistake in one of our books—maybe a mistake in the text or the code—we would be grateful if you would report this to us. By doing so, you can save other readers from frustration and help us improve subsequent versions of this book. If you find any errata, please report them by visiting `http://www.packtpub.com/submit-errata`, selecting your book, clicking on the **errata submission form** link, and entering the details of your errata. Once your errata are verified, your submission will be accepted and the errata will be uploaded on our website, or added to any list of existing errata, under the Errata section of that title. Any existing errata can be viewed by selecting your title from `http://www.packtpub.com/support`.

Piracy

Piracy of copyright material on the Internet is an ongoing problem across all media. At Packt, we take the protection of our copyright and licenses very seriously. If you come across any illegal copies of our works, in any form, on the Internet, please provide us with the location address or website name immediately so that we can pursue a remedy.

Please contact us at `copyright@packtpub.com` with a link to the suspected pirated material.

We appreciate your help in protecting our authors, and our ability to bring you valuable content.

Questions

You can contact us at `questions@packtpub.com` if you are having a problem with any aspect of the book, and we will do our best to address it.

1
Getting Started

For the past few years, web development has been growing and changing continuously, as phones are getting smarter and Internet connections, tablets, desktops, and web browsers are getting faster. Nowadays, creating and hosting a website is cheap, but creating a web app with good user experience for all device sizes and resolutions is not that easy. **AngularJS** was created for us — full stack developers, frontend developers, and/or web designers — in order to avoid wasting time repeating ourselves so that we can produce more apps with scalability, maintainability, and testability as well as apps that are developed fast enough to accomplish time to market.

There is a key AngularJS module that has been designed for animations. This AngularJS animation module's purpose is not to be a library of precreated animations but to be a way in which great AngularJS built-in tools can be easily integrated with well-known CSS3 animations and JavaScript animations, besides giving the developer the liberty to extend it for custom directives and custom animations.

In this chapter, we will cover the following topics:

- The definition of animation and the web context
- The need for AngularJS animations
- Choosing when to use JavaScript for animations
- AngularJS – combining JavaScript and CSS3

The definition of animation and the web context

Animation, by definition, is the process of creating a continuous motion over a period of time. The World Wide Web started with static HTML pages, and then .gifs and JavaScript animations started to appear. There were nonstandard <blink> and <marquee> HTML tags too, which were very annoying and limited. These were supported only by very old browsers and are currently deprecated.

Since technologies improved and the Internet bandwidth increased, animations have been a big deal on web browsers across the years. Developers started using Adobe Flash™, Java applets, Microsoft Silverlight, and other third-party solutions that lacked interoperability. Until recently, it was hard to rely 100 percent on a solution. This problem led to the creation of standards such as CSS3 Transition and CSS3 keyframe animations.

Check out `http://www.w3.org/TR/css3-animations/` and `http://www.w3.org/TR/css3-transitions/` for W3C's working drafts.

Another key improvement to animations on web browsers is the evolution of JavaScript engines and layout engines. Together, these improvements created an environment that enabled us to animate our web applications with cross-devices and the interoperability safety of operating systems. Standardization is the solution.

HTML, CSS, and JavaScript have been used to create web applications, and recently, they have even been used to create native apps for iOS, Android, and other devices with solutions such as PhoneGap.

Check out `http://phonegap.com` for more information on creating apps using web technologies.

Microsoft adopted this stack (HTML, CSS, and JavaScript) as an option in order to create native apps for Windows 8 as well. This is evidence that CSS3 and ECMAScript will evolve faster and in partnership with big companies such as Google, Microsoft, and Apple.

Currently, all major web browsers are evergreen, which means that they automatically update themselves without asking the user to accept them; they update themselves silently. This is a new era for web development. Old browsers that used poor JavaScript engines and lacked support for CSS3 are dying.

The need for AngularJS animation

AngularJS calls itself a superheroic JavaScript **Model View Whatever (MVW)** framework—no kidding; this is on the main page. AngularJS is an extensive framework that helps frontend developers on many different aspects. One of these aspects is how to animate all the stuff that magically appears on the browser when we manipulate the scope variables.

Check out the website of AngularJS at `https://angularjs.org/` for more information on this framework's awesomeness.

> The AngularJS animation module **ngAnimate** is separate from the AngularJS core module, so it's necessary to include it as a dependency of your application.

The framework is already modular as of Version 1.3 and has the intention to be even more modularized with future releases. The ngAnimate module lets you animate the common directives built in AngularJS, such as ngRepeat, ngShow, ngHide, ngIf, ngInclude, ngSwitch, and ngView.

Including the ngAnimate module in the framework enables hooks that trigger animations that you want to be displayed during the normal life cycle of native directives and custom directives.

We just need to create the animation declarations that will be triggered by these hooks using CSS3 transitions, CSS3 keyframe animations, or even JavaScript animations with callback functions. We will learn how to create these animations in *Chapter 3, Creating Our First Animation in AngularJS*.

AngularJS follows the convention of the configuration design paradigm, so animations can be placed using plain CSS3 animations just by following the naming conventions that will be listed later.

Animations on AngularJS are completely based on CSS classes. Animation hooks enabled by the ngAnimate module are provided by classes that are added or removed from elements in specific events. The events in which we can hook animations are the `enter`, `move`, and `leave` events of the DOM element and the addition or removal of a class from the element. This is a simple but powerful unique concept, as animations should be used on these events. This approach makes animations on AngularJS very intuitive without much effort or using a lot of code.

This AngularJS approach is different from jQuery animate, as we declare animations based on classes instead of imperatively adding an animation using JavaScript wherever a DOM manipulation is expected to occur. As most of these DOM manipulations are implicit in AngularJS, the animations' approach is mainly declarative and the animation hook is not intrusive.

Animations are useful for users when they grab the user's attention, catching the users' eye for specific elements, and making their lives easier. Motion builds meaning about relationships between elements, functionality, and intention of the system; it enhances the user cognition.

Animations can create responsiveness when a button element is touched and clicked on and a new element is added to the view from the origin point of the button.

Animations can tell a user when an element is moved from point A to point B of the view, guiding the user's attention. They can improve conversion; in this case, we should always use split tests.

It is easily possible to implement all the cases that I described previously using the events hooks that ngAnimate provides to us.

Google Material Design is a great resource that tells you how to apply animations to a web app. Check out `http://www.google.com/design/` for more information.

Choosing when to use JavaScript for animations

The CSS3 animations and transitions created a way for modern browsers to recognize what animations are. They also created a way for modern browsers to differentiate animations from other operations so that they can use the **Graphics Processing Unit** (**GPU**) to accelerate the hardware of the animation instead of the **Central Processing Unit** (**CPU**), which receives all other operations.

Another advantage of using CSS transitions and animations instead of JavaScript is the fact that JavaScript runs on a browser's main thread. CSS animations enable browsers to run operations on new threads and create different layers, which are separated from everything else happening on the main thread. In other words, while your main UI thread will be in heavy use, JavaScript animations might freeze although CSS animations will continue to work.

CSS3 animations, CSS3 transitions, and JavaScript animations that use `requestAnimationFrame` are the best options in order to avoid the poor performance of animations.

Nowadays, web apps run on devices too, and browsers can stop CSS3 animations when the app is in the background tab, resulting in improved battery life. This is just one of the possibilities for the browser to improve its performance. In *Chapter 8, Animations' Performance Optimization*, we will see how to optimize an animation's performance.

Check out `http://www.html5rocks.com/en/tutorials/speed/high-performance-animations/` for more information on high performance animations.

Here, we see one example of animation that can be easily created with CSS3 as well as JavaScript.

The HTML code for the page is as follows:

```
<!DOCTYPE html>
<html>
<head>
    <title>Getting Started</title>
    <link href="animations.css" rel="stylesheet" />
</head>
<body>
    <div>
        <h1>Animation with JavaScript</h1>
        <!--There is a click listener for this button -->
        <button id="jsBtn">Click here to move the element below with
JS</button>
        <div id="jsanimation">
            This block will be moved by JavaScript
        </div>
        <h1>Animation with jQuery</h1>
        <!--There is a click listener for this button -->
        <button id="jQBtn">Click here to move the element below
            with jQuery</button>
        <div id="jQanimation">
            This block will be moved by jQuery
        </div>
        <h1>Animation with CSS3 transition</h1>
        <!--There is a click listener for this button -->
        <button id="cssBtn">Click here to move the element below
            with CSS3 transition</button>
        <div id="csstransition">
```

```
                This block will be moved by CSS3 transition
        </div>
        <h1>Animation with CSS3 animation</h1>
        <!--There is a click listener for this button -->
        <button id="cssAnimationBtn">Click here to move the
            element below with CSS3 animation</button>
        <div id="cssanimation">
                This block will be moved by CSS3 animation
        </div>
    </div>
    <script src="//ajax.googleapis.com/ajax/libs/jquery/
        2.1.1/jquery.min.js"></script>
    <script src="animations.js"></script>
</body>
</html>
```

Downloading the example code

You can download the example code files for all Packt books you have purchased from your account at http://www.packtpub.com. If you purchased this book elsewhere, you can visit http://www.packtpub.com/support and register to have the files e-mailed directly to you.

The declarative way to animate is CSS. In CSS, we defined the translate transform for objects with the .move-to-right class. This declaration makes the move but does not create the animation between the moves. We declared how the div element to be moved should be transitioned; it should last 2 seconds and be slow towards the start and end.

The animations.css CSS file is as follows:

```
/* Code used by JavaScript animation sample */
#jsanimation {
    position: relative;
}


/* Code used by jQuery animation sample */
#jQanimation {
    position: relative;
}


/* Code used by CSS Transition animation sample */
#csstransition {
```

```css
    position: relative;
    /* Here we should add -moz-transition, -webkit-transition,
-o-transition for browsers compatibility, we will explain about vendor
prefixes later */
    transition: all 2s ease-in-out;
}

.move-to-right {
    /* Here we should add vendor prefixes too */
    transform: translate(100px,0);
}

/* Code used by CSS Animation sample */
#cssanimation {
    position: relative;
}

@-webkit-keyframes move-to-right-animation {
    from {
        left: 0px;
    }

    to {
        left: 100px;
    }
}

@keyframes move-to-right-animation {
    from {
        left: 0px;
    }

    to {
        left: 100px;
    }
}

.move-to-right-animation {
    position: relative;
    left: 100px;
    /* Here we should add -moz-animation, -o-animation for browsers
compatibility*/
    -webkit-animation: move-to-right-animation 1s ease-in-out;
    animation: move-to-right-animation 1s ease-in-out;
}
```

The `animations.js` JavaScript file is as follows:

```
/* Code used by JavaScript animation sample */
var jsAnimationElement = document.getElementById('jsanimation');
var jsAnimationBtn = document.getElementById('jsBtn');
/**
* Listener of the "Click here to move the element below with JS"
button
*/
jsAnimationBtn.addEventListener('click', function
moveBtnClickListener() {
    //This variable holds the position left of the div
    var positionLeft = 0;

    /**
    * function that moves jsAnimationElement 10px more to right until
the positionLeft is 100
    */
    function moveToRight() {
        positionLeft += 10;

        /* Set position left of the jsanimation div */
        jsAnimationElement.style.left = positionLeft + 'px';

        if (positionLeft < 100) {
            /* This recursive function calls itself until the object
is 100px from the left, every 100 milliseconds */
            setTimeout(moveToRight, 100);
        }
    }

    moveToRight();
}, false);

/* Code used by jQuery Animation sample */
/**
* Listener of the "Click here to move the element below with jQuery"
button
*/
$("#jQBtn").click(function () {
    /** Use the jQuery animate function to send the element to more
100px to right in 1s */
    $("#jQanimation").animate({
        left: "+=100"
    }, 1000);
```

```
});

/* Code used by CSS transition animation sample */
var cssTransitionElement = document.getElementById('csstransition');
var cssTransitionBtn = document.getElementById('cssBtn');
/**
* Listener of the "Click here to move the element below with CSS3"
button
*/
cssTransitionBtn.addEventListener('click', function
moveCssBtnClickListener() {
    /* Add class "move-to-right" to the block on button click */
    cssTransitionElement.classList.add('move-to-right');
});

/* Code used by CSS Animation sample */
var cssAnimationElement = document.getElementById('cssanimation');
var cssAnimationBtn = document.getElementById('cssAnimationBtn');
/**
* Listener of the "Click here to move the element below with CSS3"
button
*/
cssAnimationBtn.addEventListener('click', function
moveCssAnimationBtnClickListener() {
    /* Add class "move-to-right" to the block on button click */
    cssAnimationElement.classList.add('move-to-right-animation');
});
```

This code shows you four approaches for the same animation. The intention is to move a `div` element 100 px to the right smoothly. This is not the AngularJS way to create animations, but before you learn how to create an animation with AngularJS, you should know all the options.

First we created an animation with JavaScript without `requestFrameRate`. The result is not so good, and its code is not so pretty. The second animation uses jQuery animate; the code is simpler than the JavaScript version, is imperative, and the result is **OK**. The third animation uses the CSS transition; it's very clean code with a great and smooth result, declarative way. The fourth animation uses the CSS animation with the same result as the transition version. It made the animation declarative and a little more powerful than the transition, as we can add frames between 0 percent and 100 percent of the animation, although the code is bigger. At this time of writing this, it's necessary to use the `-webkit-` vendor prefix for the animation to work, even for Chrome.

Although CSS3 animations and transitions have huge advantages, they have disadvantages as well. Creating complex, combined animations is still hard or impossible in order to achieve a good result. In cases like these, JavaScript animations are a better option. JavaScript animations are an option for fallback too when transitions and CSS animations aren't available, which is a common scenario when your project supports old browsers.

A good website that will help you know which browsers have support for CSS animations and transitions is `http://caniuse.com`.

AngularJS – combining JavaScript and CSS3

AngularJS has adopted the standards for animation on the Web. It embraces CSS3 Transitions, animations, and JavaScript. It's great because the developers can choose the animation option that best fits their needs. As you have already read, sometimes, one option fits better than other, so this is a great feature of ngAnimate.

With the ngAnimate module, it is far easier to animate in AngularJS because it brings a code pattern and convention that is already integrated with AngularJS native directives. This allows us—the developers and the open source community—to have a quick start to animation and a pattern to develop our custom animations. In later chapters, we will see how to integrate custom directives with AngularJS animations using the $animate service, which is the main topic of *Chapter 5, Custom Directives and the $animate Service*.

This is all possible due to the class-bases approach that AngularJS uses. We will see more of this in *Chapter 3, Creating Our First Animation in AngularJS,* when we create our first AngularJS animation.

Another advantage is that it's easy to integrate CSS animation libraries such as `animate.css` and `Effeckt.css`, as these libraries use CSS3 transitions and animations.

Check out `http://daneden.github.io/animate.css/` and `http://h5bp.github.io/Effeckt.css/` for CSS animations libraries.

Do it yourself exercises

Create the same JavaScript animation as the one in our sample, but instead of `setTimeout`, use `requestAnimationFrame`. Check out `https://developer.mozilla.org/en-US/docs/Web/API/window.requestAnimationFrame` for more information on `requestAnimationFrame`.

Summary

In this chapter, we gave an introduction on how the AngularJS animations module and web standards work together, a notion of what can be achieved using them, and an overview of the differences between JavaScript, CSS3 animations, and transitions.

We took a quick overview of animations in web history and how attached they are to the evolution of web standards in AngularJS. We saw samples of simple animations created with JavaScript and CSS3, and we got an idea about how we should choose each one of them so that we can achieve the best performance and result.

In the next chapter, you will learn how to create animations using CSS3 in order to create smooth AngularJS animations, which are known as *jank free* animations.

2
Understanding CSS3 Transitions and Animations

CSS3 transitions and CSS3 animations are standard ways to create web animations nowadays. With only a few lines of code, we can achieve great and smooth results. In this chapter, we will learn how to use CSS3 to create the animations we want so that we can hook the animations into the AngularJS pipeline.

In this chapter, we will learn:

- CSS3 transitions
- CSS3 keyframe animations
- CSS transforms

CSS3 transitions

Before CSS3 transitions, when style properties of DOM elements were changed, web browsers applied new styles immediately after the operation, so the effects were rendered abruptly. As we saw in the last chapter, we could use JavaScript or jQuery to imperatively add a transition while changing the style. This is an option, but we already saw some reasons why CSS transitions might be a better choice. In *Chapter 8, Animation Performance Optimization*, we will learn more about the optimization of animations. CSS3 transitions enable developers to create implicit, smooth transitions when changing the CSS property of elements. We can avoid a loading animation to get frozen while JavaScript is under heavy processing by using CSS transitions. This will make a huge difference to the user's perception of quality.

Let's check a complete transition animation declaration and see how it works:

```html
<!DOCTYPE html>
<html>
<head>
    <title>Chapter 2 - First sample</title>
    <style>
        .cssanimationTimes {
            transition-property: width, background-color;
            transition-duration: 2s, 10s;
            width: 100px;
        }

        .large {
            width: 300px;
        }

        .red {
            background-color: red;
        }
    </style>
</head>
<body>
    <h1>CSS Transition animation</h1>
    <div class="cssanimationTimes">
        Element with cssanimationTimes class
    </div>
    <button id="trigger">Trigger animation</button>
    <button id="triggerReset">Reset animation</button>
    <script>
        document.getElementById('trigger').addEventListener
            ('click', function () {
        var element = document.getElementsByClassName
            ('cssanimationTimes')[0];
            //Append classes red and large, to change the background
color to red and the width to 300px
            element.className = element.className + " red large";
        });

        document.getElementById('triggerReset').addEventListener
            ('click', function () {
        var element = document.getElementsByClassName
            ('cssanimationTimes')[0];
            //Append classes red and large, to change the background
color to red and the width to 300px
```

```
            element.className = "cssanimationTimes";
        });
    </script>
</body>
</html>
```

The `cssanimationTimes` class declares that changes in the width and background color should get transitioned by the duration of 2 seconds and 10 seconds, respectively. We added the `cssanimationTimes` class to a `div` element in the DOM.

Now, we just need to replace the width or background color of the target `div` with the `cssanimationTimes` class in order to see the animation. For this, we create two buttons. The first button is the **Trigger animation** button that has a `trigger` ID. This button has a click listener that will append the `.red` and `.large` classes to our target `div` element; these classes will change the width from 100 px to 300 px and the background color from transparent to red. The second button, which is the reset button of `triggerReset` ID, just removes all other classes of the target div, leaving only the `cssanimationTimes` class.

When we click on the **Trigger animation** button, the browser already knows that the properties should be transitioned, so the animation will occur like in the upcoming sequence of screenshots.

The following page appears before you click on the **Trigger animation** button:

The following page appears 1 second after clicking on the **Trigger animation** button:

The following page appears 2 seconds after clicking on the **Trigger animation** button. At this time, the width transition is complete.

The following page appears 10 seconds after clicking on the **Trigger animation** button. At this time, the background-color transition is complete.

If we click on the **Reset animation** button, we will see the same transition as the screenshot sequence but in the reverse order. This is because the transition will apply, but this time, it will apply from the width of 300 px to 100 px and the background color will change from red to transparent.

As we saw in the last example, every transition requires a specified transition duration (`transition-duration`) and an animatable property to be transitioned (the transition property). The animatable property can be defined as `all`, so all animatable properties will be transitioned when they are changed. An animatable property is a CSS property that browsers can transition or animate. The animatable properties topic related to this property is explained later in this chapter.

In the following example, changes to any animatable property of elements with the `cssanimation` class are transitioned. This is declared as follows:

```
.cssanimation {
    transition: all 2s;
}
```

or

```
.cssanimation {
    transition-property: all;
    transition-duration: 2s;
}
```

These last samples of the CSS code define that when elements within the `cssanimation` class change in width or any other animatable property, they will transition over a period of 2 seconds.

Defining the specific transition property value instead of `all` enables us to create different transition durations for each property of the same element.

Check out this example, which is the same CSS as the first example of this chapter:

```
.cssanimationTimes {
    transition-property: width, background-color;
    transition-duration: 2s, 10s;
}
```

Also, check out the following:

```
.cssanimationTimes {
    transition: width 2s, background-color 10s;
}
```

In both these samples, when we change the width and background color at the same time, the width will have a transition duration of 2 seconds and the background color will have a transition duration of 10 seconds to complete the animations.

Here, you might think that all transitions have a constant speed between the transition duration, but we can define how the transition will behave by setting the transition timing function's property.

The transition-timing-function property

The transition timing function defines how the intermediate values used during a transition are calculated. This might change the animation speed over the function's duration, accelerating and slowing the animation.

You might want the behavior of your animations' speed as per your choice. The CSS3 transition timing function enables you to choose one of the standard speed curves (ease, linear, ease-in, and so on) that are listed, or you can define yours. This is useful because in real life, an object's movement isn't linear (constant speed), so we can simulate a natural movement by using transition timing functions. This could be different to creating a mechanical movement in order to create an interesting, familiar, and understandable movement that changes the user perception of your app transitions' aesthetics.

The default value is ease, which means that the animation effect will have a slow start, then become fast, and then end slowly.

The speed of the animation duration is commonly defined by the cubic Bézier curve. This enables great customization of the speed of the animation, if required.

 There is a great website in order to create, compare, and preview animations with different cubic Bézier curves. Check out http://cubic-bezier.com/.

To get the same effect as transition-timing-function: ease, you can define transition-timing-function: cubic-bezier (0.25, 0.1, 0.25, 1). The values ease, ease-in, ease-out, ease-in-out are just easier to use than to write the corresponding cubic Bézier curve.

The valid values for this property are as follows:

- **Ease**: This is the default value. It starts slowly, then becomes fast, and then ends slowly. The ease timing function represented as a cubic Bézier curve is displayed in the following screenshot:

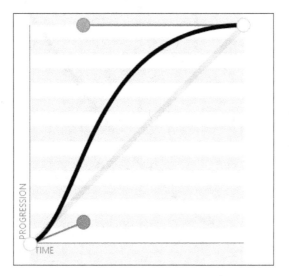

- **Linear**: This maintains the linear speed. The speed doesn't change from the start to the end. The linear timing function represented as a cubic Bézier curve is displayed in the following screenshot:

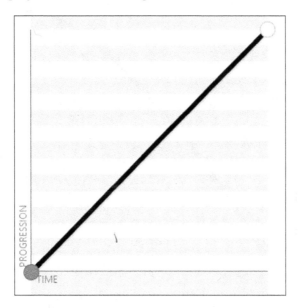

- **Ease-in**: In this, the start of the animation is slow. The ease-in timing function represented as a cubic Bézier curve is displayed as follows:

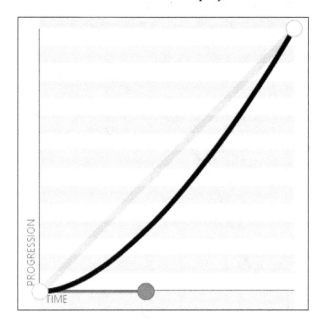

- **Ease-out**: In this, the end of the animation is slow. The ease-out timing function represented as a cubic Bézier curve is displayed in the following screenshot:

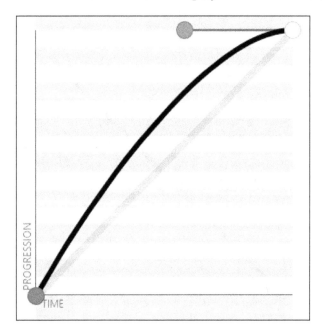

- **Ease-in-out**: In this, both the start and end of the animation are slow. The ease-in-out timing function represented as a cubic Bézier curve is displayed in the following screenshot:

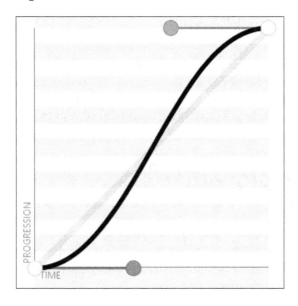

- **Step-start**: This moves to the final state of the animation at the start.
- **Step-end**: This moves to the final state of the animation only at the end.
- **steps(<integer>[,[start | end]]?)**: Steps allow us to create a segmented animation rather than a continuous animation from an initial state to a final state. It divides in *N* steps the animation (the first parameter); the second parameter is optional (the end is the default) and defines the point at which the change of values happens. The steps are often poorly understood. If you want to learn more about this, I recommend that you read this great article available at `http://designmodo.com/steps-css-animations/`; it has demos and some cases where steps are useful.
- **Cubic-bezier(<number>,<number>,<number>,<number>)**: This specifies the cubic Bézier curve. With this, you have the flexibility to create your speed curve.

 The animation demos used in all the chapters are available at the Packt Publishing website for download and testing (`www.packtpub.com`). They are also available at `https://github.com/richardkeller/AngularJS-animations-book` and `http://richardkeller.github.io/AngularJS-animations-book/`.

The transition-delay property

Another option that CSS3 transitions provide is to delay the start of an animation. The default value is 0 seconds, which means that the animation will promptly start when a property is changed. If a positive value is set, the transition will delay the execution by the time defined.

Negative values are valid too. Animations will start when the property changes as the 0s value, but it will appear to have started the animation with the value in seconds defined into the animation sequence in advance. In other words, the transition will appear to begin partway through its play cycle. It's useful to start animations midway.

Animatable properties

There are a lot of properties that can be animated using CSS Transitions and CSS animations, which are called animatable properties. It's important to know which properties can be transitioned and which values of the property can be used by an animation. The list of animatable properties is huge and almost every property that you try to animate will work. Just keep in mind that if an animation you create isn't working, check whether it's an animatable property.

The current list of animatable properties and what is animatable is available at `http://www.w3.org/TR/css3-transitions/#animatable-properties`.

Some examples of values of animatable properties are `color`, `length`, `percentage`, `calc`, and `font-weight`.

Here, we can see a sample of the HTML that will be used by three different animations using Transitions:

```
<div class="cssanimation">
       cssAnimation
</div>
<div class="cssAnimationTimesOneLine">
       cssAnimationTimesOneLine
</div>
<div class="cssanimationEasing">
       cssAnimationEasing
</div>
```

From now on, we will omit some CSS vendor-specific prefixes in order to have better clarity on the examples. We will focus on working examples for the Chrome browser, although readers can add vendor-specific prefixes to test the files on any other modern browser.

The first animation transition declaration will get animated when the width changes, as follows:

```
.cssanimation {
    width: 200px;
    border: 1px solid black;
    transition-property: width;
    transition-duration: 2s;
}

.cssanimation:hover {
    width:400px;
}
```

The second animation transition declaration will get animated when the width and background color changes, as follows:

```
.cssAnimationTimesOneLine {
    width: 100px;
    background-color: white;
    transition: width 2s, background-color 10s;
}

.cssAnimationTimesOneLine:hover {
    width: 200px;
    background-color: red;
}
```

The third animation transition declaration will get animated when all animatable properties change:

```
.cssanimationEasing {
    width: 200px;
    background-color: black;
    transition-property: all;
    transition-timing-function: ease;
    transition-duration: 2s;
}

.cssanimationEasing:hover {
    background-color: red;
}
```

The initial value of the elements is given in this figure:

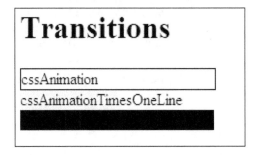

After 1 second of hovering the mouse over the `cssAnimation` element (the first item), the width is halfway there.

After 2 seconds of hovering the mouse over the `cssAnimation` element (the first item), the width is as defined in the hover declaration.

After 5 seconds of hovering the mouse over the `cssAnimationTimesOneLine` element (the second item), you can see that the color is between white and red but the width transition is already complete. This happens because we used two different durations for the transitions.

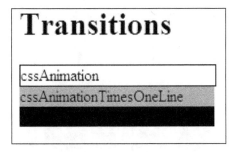

After 10 seconds of hovering the mouse over the second item, both the width and the background color are on the end of the animations, as the biggest transition was defined lasts for 10 seconds.

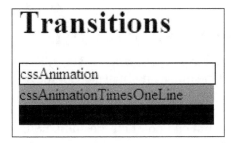

The third item hovered after 1 second. The animation of the background color is in the middle of the cycle.

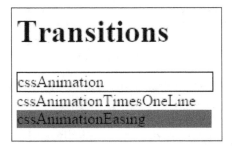

The third item hovered after 2 seconds when the animation cycle was complete:

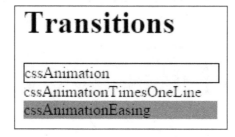

These samples showed us the result of transitioning the width and background color, and we even have different transitions in the same element.

CSS3 keyframe animations

CSS transitions allowed us to create animations using CSS for the first time. With CSS Transitions, we can define the initial and final state of the transition animation, but the progress in between the transition duration is a little out of control. It is just controlled using the `transition-timing-function` and `transition-delay` properties. This enables us to define a start and end point for the animation, and the transition connects these together. What if we want to create an animation with multiple steps and take a nonlinear path in between the start and end of the animation?

CSS keyframe animations allow us to create multiple steps between an animation duration with different timing functions between these steps. This makes our life easy as it creates complex animations using the concept of keyframes; otherwise, we will have to create multiple transitions in a sequence in order to create the full animation. In other words, transitions are a subset of what we can do using CSS keyframes.

CSS animations give developers more control over the animation's progress-defining keyframes. A keyframe is the explicit definition of the element style in a specific phase of the animation in between the animation progress. This is a different approach from transitions; transition keyframes are defined implicitly, and animation keyframes are defined explicitly.

Defining an animation using keyframes

The definition of an animation using keyframes is different from the transition definition.

First, we declare the animation states between the animation time on a `@keyframes` rule.

The keyframe can be defined using the `from` and `to` keywords or using a list of percentages, so the definition is relative to the animation duration. Here are two samples of valid keyframe declaration:

```
@-webkit-keyframes first-animation {
    from {
        border-color:blue;
    }

    to {
        border-color:red;
    }
}



@keyframes first-animation {
    from {
        border-color:blue;
    }

    to {
        border-color:red;
    }
}
```

Also, take a look at the following example:

```
@-webkit-keyframes first-animation-percentage {
    0% {
        border-color: blue;
    }

    100% {
        border-color: red;
    }
}


@keyframes first-animation-percentage {
    0% {
        border-color: blue;
    }

    100% {
        border-color: red;
    }
}
```

So far, it seems clear that we defined the property value for the beginning and end of an animation using both approaches of percentage and keywords. Using CSS Animations, unlike CSS Transitions, we can add multiple steps using keyframes' percentage definitions for a single CSS animation. However, which elements will display the declared animation?

We define the animation that should be triggered on the element selector by adding the `animation-name` property with the keyframes' name as the value or a list of keyframes if we want to apply more than one animation to the same selector.

Here, we have a sample that applies the `first-animation` CSS animation to elements with the `animationOne` class:

```
.animationOne {
    border: 2px solid black;

    -webkit-animation-name:first-animation;
    animation-name:first-animation;

    -webkit-animation-duration:5s;
    animation-duration: 5s;
}
```

As the preceding example shows, there is an animation-duration property that defines how long the animation lasts once it is triggered.

The animation will be displayed as soon the page is loaded or when the animation is defined for an element.

Before the animation, this is what appears:

After 5 seconds of the animation, this is what appears:

Separating timing functions for each keyframe interval

Another cool feature of CSS animations is that we can set the timing function like we could on CSS transitions, but we can choose one different timing function for each keyframe interval as well.

Here, we have a sample:

```
@keyframes second-animation-timing {
    0% {
        animation-timing-function:ease-in;
    }

    25% {
        transform:translateX(50px);
        animation-timing-function:ease-out;
    }

    50% {
        transform:translateX(100px);
        animation-timing-function:linear;
    }

    100% {
        transform:translateX(200px);
    }
}
```

The first percentage determines `animation-timing-function` until the next percentage, and so on until the last percentage. In the sample, the animation will be displayed as the `ease-in` timing from 0 percent to 25 percent, the `ease-out` timing from 25 percent to 50 percent, and the `linear` timing from 50 percent to 100 percent.

To facilitate the coding of CSS animations, we need to use preprocessors such as LESS and SASS. With CSS preprocessors, we can use mixins in order to avoid missing out on some vendor-specific properties and duplicate less code.

I won't use mixins in my samples to show pure CSS. However, I wouldn't start a web app nowadays without using CSS preprocessors; they are really useful.

Another option is to use the Grunt task auto-prefixer.

Other CSS keyframe animations' properties

There are some more animation properties listed as follows:

- **The animation-fill-mode**: This is a way to change the elements' properties to a value other than the original one; animations don't change the elements' property values because the default value of the animation-fill-mode is none. So, when the animation is complete, the animated element returns to the original state and property values. This is the reason why the last animations' samples return to the initial state. There is a great video on the animation-fill-mode at http://www.valhead.com/2013/01/04/tutorial-css-animation-fill-mode/.

- **The animation-iteration-count**: CSS keyframe animations have the animation-iteration-count property that determines how many times the animation cycle will repeat; the default value is 1. You can use noninteger values too in order to have an animation that only has a partial cycle, without displaying the whole animation sequence. Even "infinite" values are allowed so that you can create infinite loops for animations.

- **The animation-direction**: We can create reversed animations using the animation-direction property. The valid values are normal (the default value), reverse (so the animation is rendered backwards), alternate (which will display one cycle frontwards and the other backwards), and alternate-reverse is the same as alternate but the first cycle is reversed instead of normal. This is useful because we can avoid creating two animations when we only want to display the same animation, but backwards, this is just a property change instead of creating two animations.

- **The animation-delay**: The animation-delay property exists and behaves in the same way as the transition-delay. If we set the animation-fill-mode to forwards, the animated element properties after the animation ends are set to the last value determined by the animation, which might be different from the original values, as this comes from the "from" values when the animation-direction is normal. If the value is defined backwards, the value set while the animation is on animation-delay time is the same from the beginning of the animation; the "from" in the case of the animation-direction is normal. There is a value called both too, which makes the animation behave in such a way as if backwards and forwards were set.

- **The animation-play-state**: Another useful property is the animation-play-state. This property can be dynamically set to paused so that it pauses the execution, and after that, it can be set to running so that it continues to run from the last state. This allows us to control the animation state using JavaScript.

There is a cool tool where you can create CSS animations and preview them available at http://cssanimate.com.

CSS3 transforms

Now that we know how to declare an animation either by CSS Transitions or by CSS Animations, we will learn how to transform elements so that we will get able to create cool and useful animations.

CSS transforms allow us to transform an element by scaling, skewing, translating, or rotating it in two or three dimensions.

Here, you can imagine how to use a transform with our animations and transitions. The good news is that transform is an animatable property, which means that we can use this feature with keyframes and transitions in order to achieve animation effects. Transforms aren't strictly used for animations, but they are often useful in combination with animations.

This method is useful because it's relative, it's generic, and it can be reused on many occasions. If we want to scale an item to two times its size, we can use it for an element with a width of 100 px or 1000 px. The size doesn't matter, it will just double it. The same applies to moving elements using `translate`; it's better than to change the absolute values of the top, right, bottom, and left values using `translate`. The element will move relatively, independent of its initial state.

This follows the AngularJS philosophy of declaratively creating reusable components that can be used across different contexts rather than writing imperative code that only works in a particular situation.

A CSS transform can be declared as follows:

```
.transformOne {
    display: block;
    width: 50px;
    height: 50px;
    border: 1px solid black;
}

.transformOne:hover {
    -webkit-transform: rotate(90deg);
    transform: rotate(90deg);
}
```

Although the element will be rotated 90 degrees clockwise when the `transformOne` element is hovered, it won't be smooth.

The result of the last sample before the hovering is as follows:

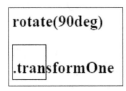

The result of the last sample after the hover is as follows:

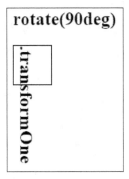

To create a smooth rotate animation, we can integrate CSS Transform and CSS Transition, as shown in the following sample:

```
.transformTwo {
    display: block;
    width: 50px;
    height: 50px;
    border: 1px solid black;
    -webkit-transition: -webkit-transform ease-in 1s;
    transition: transform ease-in 1s;
}

.transformTwo:hover {
    -webkit-transform: rotate(90deg);
    transform: rotate(90deg);
}
```

The following is the result of the last sample before the hover:

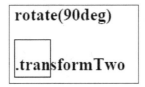

The following is the result of the last sample 0.5 seconds after the hover:

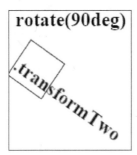

The following is the result of the last sample after the hover:

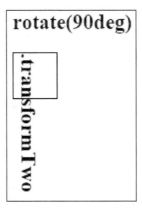

In the last example, we added a transition to the element, so the transform will be transitioned for one second on the hover, as we can see in the preceding images.

A similar transform rotate can be applied using the CSS animation, as follows:

```
@-webkit-keyframes animation-transform {
    from {
        -webkit-transform:rotate(0deg);
        transform: rotate(0deg);
    }

    50% {
        -webkit-transform: rotate(90deg);
        transform: rotate(90deg);
    }

    to {
        -webkit-transform: rotate(360deg);
        transform: rotate(360deg);
    }
}

@keyframes animation-transform {
    from {
        transform: rotate(0deg);
    }

    50% {
        transform: rotate(90deg);
    }

    to {
        transform: rotate(360deg);
    }
}

.transformThree {
    display: block;
    width: 100px;
    height: 50px;
    border: 1px solid red;
    -webkit-animation-name: animation-transform;
    animation-name: animation-transform;
    -webkit-animation-duration: 5s;
    animation-duration: 5s;
}
```

This last sample showed us an animation of an element that rotates 360 degrees in two phases: 90 degrees on the first half of the execution and until 360 degrees on the second half. Creating this animation in JavaScript can be complex, or it would not be as easy as it is on CSS at least, and wouldn't be as smooth as it is on CSS.

Now, we have the power to create animations that we will use on AngularJS directives as well.

The transform accepts beyond `rotate()` values as `scale()`, `translate()`, `skew()`, and the relative one-axis functions: `translateX()`, `translateY()`, `scaleX()`, `scaleY()`, `skewX()`, and `skewY()`.

The scale function

The scale function is used to scale elements in proportion to the original size.

The `scale(1)` value is the original size, `scale(0.5)` will be half the size, and `scale(2)` will be double the original size.

In the following sample, we will see how to double the size of an image in both the x and y axis just by hovering it:

```
.transformFour img:hover {
    -webkit-transform: scale(2);
    transform: scale(2);
}
```

The `Scale()` function accepts two parameters if we use both x and y axes. The first one is relative to the x axis, and the second one is relative to the y axis. We can deform the image using `scale` with two parameters; this is a little-used feature that can produce fun, interesting effects, as shown in the following sample:

```
.transformFive img:hover {
    -webkit-transform: scale(2,1);
    transform: scale(2,1);
}
```

Check the `transformFive` element before hovering your mouse over it:

The AngularJS shield logo, provided by the AngularJS team at `https://github.` `com/angular/angular.js/tree/master/images/logo`, is licensed under the Creative Commons Attribution-ShareAlike 3.0 Unported License (`http://` `creativecommons.org/licenses/by-sa/3.0/`).

Check the `transformFive` element after hovering your mouse over it:

In this sample, just the x axis of the image has been doubled; the y axis will keep its original size.

If you prefer, you can still use the `scaleX()` and `scaleY()` functions; each one scales the element to its corresponding axis. This means that `transform: scale(1,3);` has the same result as `transform:scaleY(3)` combined with `scaleX(1)`.

The translate function

The `translate` function allows us to move one element on the x and y axis.

If we define `transform: translate(100px,50px)` in an element, it will be moved 100 px on the x axis and 50 px on the y axis.

If we define `transform: translate(100px)` in an element, it will be moved 100 px on the x axis, and the second parameter is optional.

Another possibility is to use axis-specific functions, such as `translateX()` and `translateY()`.

If we define `transform: translateX(100px)` in an element, it will be moved 100 px on the *x* axis.

Check out the `translateX(100px)` effect in the following sample:

```
.transformTranslate {
    display: block;
    width: 400px;
    height: 50px;
    border: 1px solid red;
    background-color: grey;
}
.transformTranslate:hover {
    -webkit-transform: translateX(100px);
    transform: translateX(100px);
}
```

Before the execution of `translateX(100px)`, the following screenshot appears:

transform: translateX(100px)

.transformTranslate

After hovering your mouse over the element when `translateX(100px)` is applied, the following screenshot will appear:

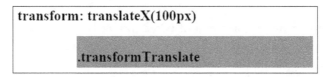

transform: translateX(100px)

.transformTranslate

If we define `transform: translateY(100px)` in an element, it will be moved 100 px on the *y* axis.

The skew function

The skew function is used to lean the element in one direction or another. The skew function parameters expect angles to be leaned, and values such as 45deg are valid.

We should use skewX() and skewY() only in order to skew around the respective axis by the angle passed as the parameter.

One sample of skew of 45 degrees on *x* axis is as follows:

```
.transformSix {
    display: block;
    width: 100px;
    height: 50px;
    border: 1px solid red;
    background-color: grey;
}

.transformSix:hover {
    -webkit-transform: skewX(45deg);
    transform: skewX(45deg);
}
```

The result before the skew is applied is as follows:

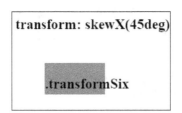

The result after hovering on the element when skewX(45deg) is applied is as follows:

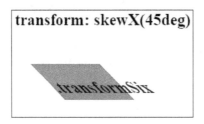

Exercise

1. Create one simple loading animation using three `div` elements that contain an animation. Each one should be filled by a black background color that increases the size from 0 to 20 px in height and width in a sequence. So, the first animation starts first, the second has a longer delay than the first one, and the third has more delay than the second one in an infinite loop.

2. Create a loading animation using `transform:rotate` and CSS animations.

3. Create an animation of a ball image or a circle that goes 100px to the right, gets back 50 px to the left, and goes 150 px to the right — all in a single animation.

4. Create the same animation as the one in exercise 2 but in the reverse order.

5. Create two animations similar to the animations in the guidelines of Google Material Design described at `http://www.google.com/design/spec/animation/authentic-motion.html#`

Summary

With the CSS3 specifications learned in this chapter, we should now be able to create simple-to-medium complex animations using CSS transitions, CSS animations, and CSS transforms. We can create loading spins, move elements smoothly, create animations with the timing we want as long as we want and professionally decide when to use CSS Transition or CSS Animation for a specific animation.

We are now ready to create our first animation on AngularJS, which will be the topic of the next chapter.

3
Creating Our First Animation in AngularJS

Now that we know how to create CSS animations, we will learn how to apply them within the context of AngularJS by creating animations using CSS transitions and CSS keyframe animations that are integrated with AngularJS native directives using the ngAnimate module. The later chapters will cover custom directives and JavaScript animations integrated with AngularJS as well.

In this chapter, we will learn:

- The ngAnimate module setup and usage
- AngularJS directives with support for out-of-the-box animation
- AngularJS animations with the CSS transition
- AngularJS animations with CSS keyframe animations
- The naming convention of the CSS animation classes
- Animation of the ngMessage and ngMessages directives

The ngAnimate module setup and usage

AngularJS is a module-based framework; if we want our AngularJS application to have the animation feature, we need to add the animation module (ngAnimate). We have to include this module in the application by adding the module as a dependency in our AngularJS application.

However, before that, we should include the JavaScript angular-animate.js file in HTML. Both files are available on the Google **content distribution network (CDN)**, Bower, Google Code, and https://angularjs.org/.

The Google developers CDN hosts many versions of AngularJS, as listed here:

`https://developers.google.com/speed/libraries/devguide#angularjs`

Currently, AngularJS Version 1.3.0 is the latest stable version, so we will use AngularJS Version 1.3.0 on all sample files of this book; we can get them from `https://ajax.googleapis.com/ajax/libs/angularjs/1.3.0/angular.min.js` and `https://ajax.googleapis.com/ajax/libs/angularjs/1.3.0/angular-animate.min.js`.

> You might want to use Bower. To do so, check out this great video article at `https://thinkster.io/egghead/intro-to-bower/`, explaining how to use Bower to get AngularJS.

We include the JavaScript files of AngularJS and the `ngAnimate` module, and then we include the `ngAnimate` module as a dependency of our app. This is shown in the following sample, using the Google CDN and the minified versions of both files:

```html
<!DOCTYPE html>
<html ng-app"myApp">
<head>
  <title>AngularJS animation installation</title>
</head>
<body>
  <script src="//ajax.googleapis.com/ajax/libs/angularjs/
    1.3.0/angular.min.js"></script>
  <script src="//ajax.googleapis.com/ajax/libs/angularjs/
    1.3.0/angular-animate.min.js"></script>
  <script>
    var app = angular.module('myApp', ['ngAnimate']);
  </script>
</body>
</html>
```

Here, we already have an AngularJS web app configured to use animations. Now, we will learn how to animate using AngularJS directives.

AngularJS directives with native support for animations

AngularJS has the purpose of changing the way web developers and designers manipulate the **Document Object Model (DOM)**. We don't directly manipulate the DOM when developing controllers, services, and templates. AngularJS does all the DOM manipulation work for us. The only place where an application touches the DOM is within directives. For most of the DOM manipulation requirements, AngularJS already provides built-in directives that fit our needs. There are many important AngularJS directives that already have built-in support for animations, and they use the ngAnimate module. This is why this module is so useful; it allows us to use animations within AngularJS directives DOM manipulation. This way, we don't have to replicate native directives by extending them just to add animation functionality.

The ngAnimate module provides us a way to hook animations in between AngularJS directives execution. It even allows us to hook on custom directives. This will be the main topic of *Chapter 5, Custom Directives and the $animate Service*.

As we are dealing with animations between DOM manipulations, we can have animations before and after an element is added to or removed from the DOM, after an element changes (by adding or removing classes), and before and after an element is moved in the DOM. These events are the moments when we might add animations.

Fade animations using AngularJS

Now that we already know how to install a web app with the ngAnimate module enabled, let's create fade-in and fade-out animations to get started with AngularJS animations.

We will use the same HTML from the installation topic and add a simple controller, just to change an ngShow directive model value and add a CSS transition.

The ngShow directive shows or hides the given element based on the expression provided to the ng-show attribute.

For this sample, we have a **Toggle fade** button that changes the ngShow model value, so we can see what happens when the element fades in and fades out from the DOM. The ngShow directive shows and hides an element by adding and removing the ng-hide class from the element that contains the directive, shown as follows:

```
<!DOCTYPE html>
<html ng-app="myApp">
<head>
  <title>AngularJS animation installation</title>
```

```
    </head>
    <body>
      <style type="text/css">
        .firstSampleAnimation.ng-hide-add,
        .firstSampleAnimation.ng-hide-remove {
          -webkit-transition: 1s ease-in-out opacity;
          transition: 1s ease-in-out opacity;
          opacity: 1;
        }

        .firstSampleAnimation.ng-hide {
          opacity: 0;
        }
      </style>
      <div>
        <div ng-controller="animationsCtrl">
          <h1>ngShow animation</h1>
          <button ng-click="fadeAnimation =
            !fadeAnimation">Toggle fade</button>
          fadeAnimation value: {{fadeAnimation}}
          <div class="firstSampleAnimation" ng-show="fadeAnimation">
            This element appears when the fadeAnimation model
              is true
          </div>
        </div>
      </div>
      <script src="//ajax.googleapis.com/ajax/libs/angularjs/
        1.3.0/angular.min.js"></script>
      <script src="//ajax.googleapis.com/ajax/libs/angularjs/
        1.3.0/angular-animate.min.js"></script>
      <script>
      var app = angular.module('myApp', ['ngAnimate']);
      app.controller('animationsCtrl', function ($scope) {
        $scope.fadeAnimation = false;
      });
    </script>
  </body>
</html>
```

In the CSS code, we declared an opacity transition to elements with the firstAnimationSample and ng-hide-add classes, or elements with the firstAnimationSample and ng-hide-remove classes.

We also added the firstAnimationSample class to the same element that has the ng-show directive attribute.

The `fadeAnimation` model is initially `false`, so the element with the `ngShow` directive is initially hidden, as the `ngShow` directive adds the `ng-hide` class to the element to set the display property as `none`.

When we first click on the **Toggle fade** button, the `fadeAnimation` model will become `true`. Then, the `ngShow` directive will remove the `ng-hide` class to display the element. But before that, the `ngAnimate` module knows there is a transition declared for this element. Because of that, the `ngAnimate` module will append the `ng-hide-remove` class to trigger the hide animation.

Then, `ngAnimate` will add the `ng-hide-remove-active` class that can contain the final state of the animation to the element and remove the `ng-hide` class at the same time. Both classes will last until the animation (1 second in this sample) finishes, and then they are removed. This is the fade-in animation; `ngAnimate` triggers animations by adding and removing the classes that contain the animations; this is why we say that AngularJS animations are class based.

This is where the magic happens. All that we did to create this fade-in animation was declare a CSS transition with the class name `ng-hide-remove`. This class name means that it's appended when the `ng-hide` class is removed.

The fade-out animation will happen when we click on the **Toggle fade** button again, and then, the `fadeAnimation` model will become `false`. The `ngShow` directive will add the `ng-hide` class to remove the element, but before this, the `ngAnimate` module knows that there is a transition declared for that element too. The `ngAnimate` module will append the `ng-hide-add` class and then add the `ng-hide` and `ng-hide-add-active` classes to the element at the same time. Both classes will last until the animation (1 second in this sample) finishes, then they are removed, and only the `ng-hide` class is kept to hide the element.

The fade-out animation was created by just declaring the CSS transition with the class name `ng-hide-add`. It is easy to understand that this class is appended to the element when the `ng-hide` class is about to be added.

The AngularJS animations convention

As this chapter is intended to teach you how to create animations with AngularJS, you need to know which directives already have built-in support for AngularJS animations to make your life easier.

Here, we have a table of directives with the directive names and the events of the directive life cycle when animation hooks are supported.

The first row means that the `ngRepeat` directive supports animation on enter, leave, and move event times.

All events are relative to DOM manipulations, for example, when an element enters or leaves the DOM, or when a class is added to or removed from an element.

Directive	Supported animations
ngRepeat	Enter, leave, and move
ngView	Enter and leave
ngInclude	Enter and leave
ngSwitch	Enter and leave
ngIf	Enter and leave
ngClass	Add and remove
ngShow and ngHide	Add and remove
form and ngModel	Add and remove
ngMessages	Add and remove
ngMessage	Enter and leave

Perhaps the more experienced AngularJS users have noticed that the most frequently used directives are attended in this list. This is great; it means that animating with AngularJS isn't hard for most use cases.

AngularJS animation with CSS transitions

We need to know how to bind the CSS animation we learned about in *Chapter 2, Understanding CSS3 Transitions and Animations,* as well as the AngularJS directives listed in the previous table. The ngIf directive, for example, has support for the enter and leave animations.

When the value of the ngIf model is changed to true, it triggers the animation by adding the ng-enter class to the element just after the ngIf DOM element is created and injected. This triggers the animation, and the classes are kept for the duration of the transition. Then, the ng-enter class is removed. When the value of ngIf is changed to false, the ng-leave class is added to the element just before the ngIf content is removed from the DOM, and so, the animation is triggered while the element still exists.

To illustrate the AngularJS ngIf directive and ngAnimate module behavior, let's see what happens in a sample.

First, we have to declare a button that toggles the value of the `fadeAnimation` model and one `div` tag that uses `ng-if="fadeAnimation"` so we can see what happens when the element is removed and added back.

Here, we create the HTML code using the HTML template we used in the last topic to install the `ngAnimate` module:

```html
<!DOCTYPE html>
<html ng-app="myApp">
<head>
    <title>AngularJS ngIf sample</title>
</head>
<body>
    <style>
        /* ngIf animation */
        .animationIf.ng-enter,
        .animationIf.ng-leave {
            -webkit-transition: opacity ease-in-out 1s;
            transition: opacity ease-in-out 1s;
        }

        .animationIf.ng-enter,
        .animationIf.ng-leave.ng-leave-active {
            opacity: 0;
        }

        .animationIf.ng-leave,
        .animationIf.ng-enter.ng-enter-active {
            opacity: 1;
        }
    </style>
    <div ng-controller="animationsCtrl">
        <h1>ngIf animation</h1>
        <div>
            fadeAnimation value: {{fadeAnimation}}
        </div>
        <button ng-click="fadeAnimation = !fadeAnimation">
          Toggle fade</button>
        <div ng-if="fadeAnimation" class="animationIf">
            This element appears when the fadeAnimation model is true
        </div>
    </div>
    <script src="//ajax.googleapis.com/ajax/libs/angularjs
      /1.3.0/angular.min.js"></script>
    <script src="//ajax.googleapis.com/ajax/libs/angularjs
      /1.3.0/angular-animate.min.js"></script>
    <script>
```

```
        var app = angular.module('myApp', ['ngAnimate']);
        app.controller('animationsCtrl', function ($scope) {
            $scope.fadeAnimation = false;
        });
    </script>
</body>
</html>
```

So, let's see what happens in the DOM just after we click on the **Toggle fade** button. We will use **Chrome Developer Tools (Chrome DevTools)** to check the HTML in each animation step. It's a native tool that comes with the Chrome browser. To open Chrome DevTools, you just need to right-click on any part of the page and click on **Inspect Element**.

The ng-enter class

Our CSS declaration added an animation to the element with the `animationIf` and `ng-enter` classes. So, the transition is applied when the element has the `ng-enter` class too. This class is appended to the element when the element has just entered the DOM. It's important to add the specific class of the element you want to animate in the selector, which in this case is the `animationIf` class, because many other elements might trigger animation and add the `ng-enter` class too. We should be careful to use the specific target element class.

Until the animation is completed, the resulting HTML fragment will be as follows:

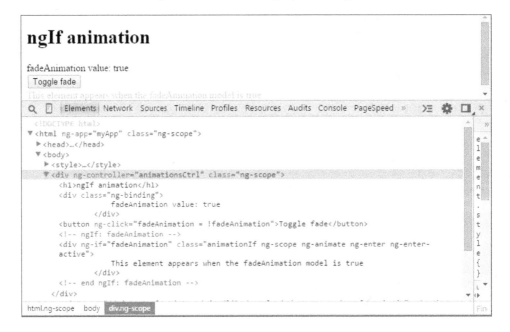

Consider the following snippet:

```
<div ng-if="fadeAnimation" class="animationIf ng-scope
  ng-animate ng-enter ng-enter-active">
  fadeAnimation value: true
</div>
```

We can see that the `ng-animate`, `ng-enter`, and `ng-enter-active` classes were added to the element.

After the animation is completed, the DOM will have the animation classes removed as the next screenshot shows:

As you can see, the animation classes are removed:

```
<div ng-if="fadeAnimation" class="animationIf ng-scope">
  This element appears when the fadeAnimation model is true
</div>
```

The ng-leave class

We added the same transition of the ng-enter class to the element with the
animationIf and ng-leave classes. The ng-leave class is added to the element
before the element leaves the DOM. So, before the element vanishes, it will display
the fade effect too.

If we click again on the **Toggle fade** button, the leave animation will be displayed
and the following HTML fragment and screen will be rendered:

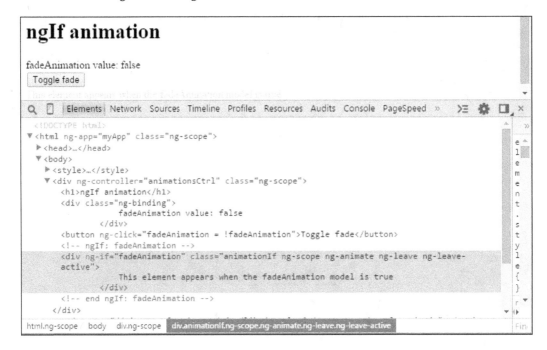

The fragment rendered is as follows:

```
<div ng-if="fadeAnimation" class="animationIf ng-scope
   g-animate ng-leave ng-leave-active">
   This element appears when the fadeAnimation model is true
</div>
```

We can notice that the ng-animate, ng-leave, and ng-leave-active classes were
added to the element.

Finally, after the element is removed from the DOM, the rendered result will be as follows:

The code after removing the element is as follows:

```
<div ng-controller="animationsCtrl" class="ng-scope">
  <div class="ng-binding">
    fadeAnimation value: false
  </div>
  <button ng-click="fadeAnimation = !fadeAnimation">
    Toggle fade</button>
  <!-- ngIf: fadeAnimation -->
</div>
```

Furthermore, there are the `ng-enter-active` and `ng-leave-active` classes. They are appended to the element classes too. Both are used to define the target value of the transition, and the `-active` classes define the destination CSS so that we can create a transition between the start and the end of an event. For example, `ng-enter` is the initial class of the enter event and `ng-enter-active` is the final class of the enter event. They are used to determine the style applied at the start of the animation and the final transition style, and they are displayed when the transition completes the cycle. A use case of the `-active` class is when we want to set an initial color and a final color using the CSS transition.

In the last sample case, the `ng-leave` class has `opacity` set to `1` and the `ng-leave-active` class has `opacity` set to `0`; so, the element will fade away at the end of the animation.

Great, we just created our first animation using AngularJS and CSS transitions.

AngularJS animation with CSS keyframe animations

We created an animation using the `ngIf` directive and CSS transitions. Now we are going to create an animation using `ngRepeat` and CSS animations (keyframes).

As we saw in the earlier table on directives and the supported animation events, the `ngRepeat` directive supports animation on the enter, leave, and move events. We already used the enter and leave events in the last sample. The move event is triggered when an item is moved around on the list of items.

For this sample, we will create three functions on the controller scope: one to add elements to the list in order to execute the enter event, one to remove an item from the list in order to execute the leave event, and one to sort the elements so that we can see the move event.

Here is the JavaScript with the functions; `$scope.items` is the array that we will use on the `ngRepeat` directive:

```javascript
var app = angular.module('myApp', ['ngAnimate']);
  app.controller('animationsCtrl', function ($scope) {
    $scope.items = [{ name: 'Richard' }, { name: 'Bruno' }
      , { name: 'Jobson' }];
    $scope.counter = 0;
    $scope.addItem = function () {
      var name = 'Item' + $scope.counter++;
      $scope.items.push({ name: name });
    };
    $scope.removeItem = function () {
      var length = $scope.items.length;
      var indexRemoved = Math.floor(Math.random() * length);
      $scope.items.splice(indexRemoved, 1);
    };
    $scope.sortItems = function () {
      $scope.items.sort(function (a, b) { return a[name]
        < b[name] ? -1 : 1 });
    };
  });
```

The HTML is as follows; it is without the CSS styles because we will see them later separating each animation block:

```
<!DOCTYPE html>
<html ng-app="myApp">
<head>
  <title>AngularJS ngRepeat sample</title>
</head>
<body>
  <div ng-controller="animationsCtrl">
    <h1>ngRepeat Animation</h1>
    <div>
      <div ng-repeat="item in items" class="repeatItem">
        {{item.name}}
      </div>
      <button ng-click="addItem()">Add item</button>
        <button ng-click="removeItem()">Remove
        item</button><button ng-click="sortItems()">
        Sort items</button>
    </div>
  </div>
  <script src="//ajax.googleapis.com/ajax/libs/angularjs
    /1.3.0/angular.min.js"></script>
  <script src="//ajax.googleapis.com/ajax/libs/angularjs
    /1.3.0/angular-animate.min.js"></script>
</body>
</html>
```

We will add an animation to the element with the `repeatItem` and `ng-enter` classes, and we will declare the `from` and `to` keyframes. So, when an element appears, it starts with `opacity` set to `0` and `color` set as `red` and will animate for 1 second until `opacity` is `1` and `color` is `black`. This will be seen when an item is added to the `ngRepeat` array.

The enter animation definition is declared as follows:

```
/* ngRepeat ng-enter animation */
.repeatItem.ng-enter {
  -webkit-animation: 1s ng-enter-repeat-animation;
  animation: 1s ng-enter-repeat-animation;
}
@-webkit-keyframes ng-enter-repeat-animation {
  from {
    opacity: 0;
    color: red;
  }
```

```
    to {
      opacity: 1;
      color: black;
    }
  }
}
@keyframes ng-enter-repeat-animation {
  from {
    opacity: 0;
    color: red;
  }
  to {
    opacity: 1;
    color: black;
  }
}
```

The move animation is declared next, to be triggered when we move an item of ngRepeat. We will add a keyframe animation to the element with the repeatItem and ng-move classes. We will declare the from and to keyframes; so, when an element moves, it starts with opacity set to 0 and color set as black and will animate for 1 second until opacity is 0.5 and color is blue, shown as follows:

```
/* ngRepeat ng-move animation */
.repeatItem.ng-move {
  -webkit-animation: 1s ng-move-repeat-animation;
  animation: 1s ng-move-repeat-animation;
}
@-webkit-keyframes ng-move-repeat-animation {
  from {
    opacity: 1;
    color: black;
  }
  to {
    opacity: 0.5;
    color: blue;
  }
}
@keyframes ng-move-repeat-animation {
  from {
    opacity: 1;
    color: black;
  }
```

```
    to {
      opacity: 0.5;
      color: blue;
    }
  }
```

The leave animation is declared next and is to be triggered when we remove an item of ngRepeat. We will add a keyframe animation to the element with the repeatItem and ng-leave classes; we will declare the from and to keyframes. So, when an element leaves the DOM, it starts with opacity set to 1 and color set as black and animates for 1 second until opacity is 0 and color is red, shown as follows:

```
/* ngRepeat ng-leave animation */
.repeatItem.ng-leave {
  -webkit-animation: 1s ng-leave-repeat-animation;
  animation: 1s ng-leave-repeat-animation;
}
@-webkit-keyframes ng-leave-repeat-animation {
  from {
    opacity: 1;
    color: black;
  }
  to {
    opacity: 0;
    color: red;
  }
}
@keyframes ng-leave-repeat-animation {
  from {
    opacity: 1;
    color: black;
  }
  to {
    opacity: 0;
    color: red;
  }
}
```

We can see that the ng-enter-active and ng-leave-active classes aren't used on this sample, as the keyframe animation already determines the initial and final properties' states. In this case, as we used CSS keyframes, the classes with the -active suffix are useless, although for CSS transitions, it's useful to set an animation destination.

The CSS naming convention

In the last few sections, we saw how to create animations using AngularJS, CSS transitions, and CSS keyframe animations. Creating animations using both CSS transitions and CSS animations is very similar because all animations in AngularJS are class based, and AngularJS animations have a well-defined class name pattern.

We must follow the CSS naming convention by adding a specific class to the directive element so that we can determine the element animation. Otherwise, the ngAnimate module will not be able to recognize which element the animation applies to.

We already know that both ngIf and ngRepeat use the ng-enter, ng-enter-active, ng-leave, and ng-leave-active classes that are added to the element in the enter and leave events. It's the same naming convention used by the ngInclude, ngSwitch, ngMessage, and ngView directives.

The ngHide and ngShow directives follow a different convention. They add the ng-hide-add and ng-hide-add-active classes when the element is going to be hidden. When the element is going to be shown, they add the ng-hide-remove and ng-hide-remove-active classes. These class names are more intuitive for the purpose of hiding and showing elements. There is also the ngClass directive convention that uses the class name added to create the animation classes with the -add, -add-active, -remove, and -remove-active suffixes, similar to the ngHide directive.

The ngRepeat directive uses the ng-move and ng-move-active classes when elements move position in the DOM, as we already saw in the last sample.

The ngClass directive animation sample

The ngClass directive allows us to dynamically set CSS classes. So, we can programmatically add and remove CSS from DOM elements. Classes are already used to change element styles, so it's good to see how useful animating the ngClass directive is.

Let's see a sample of ngClass so that it's easier to understand.

We will create the HTML code with a **Toggle ngClass** button that will add and remove the animationClass class from the element with the initialClass class through the ngClass directive:

```
<!DOCTYPE html>
<html ng-app="myApp">
<head>
```

```
        <title>AngularJS ngClass sample</title>
    </head>
    <body>
        <link href="ngClassSample.css" rel="stylesheet" />
        <div>
            <h1>ngClass Animation</h1>
            <div>
                <button ng-click="toggleNgClass = !toggleNgClass">Toggle
    ngClass</button>
                <div class="initialClass" ng-class="
                  {'animationClass' : toggleNgClass}">
                    This element has class 'initialClass' and
                        the ngClass directive is declared as
                        ng-class="{'animationClass' : toggleNgClass}"
                </div>
            </div>
        </div>
        <script src="//ajax.googleapis.com/ajax/libs/angularjs
          /1.3.0/angular.min.js"></script>
        <script src="//ajax.googleapis.com/ajax/libs/angularjs
          /1.3.0/angular-animate.min.js"></script>
        <script>
            var app = angular.module('myApp', ['ngAnimate']);
        </script>
    </body>
</html>
```

For this sample, we will use two basic classes: an initial class and the class that the ngClass directive will add to and remove from the element:

```
/* ngclass animation */
/*This is the initialClass, that keeps in the element*/
.initialClass {
    background-color: white;
    color: black;
    border: 1px solid black;
}
/* This is the animationClass, that is added or removed by the ngClass
expression*/
.animationClass {
    background-color: black;
    color: white;
    border: 1px solid white;
}
```

To create the animation, we will define a CSS animation using keyframes; so, we only need to use the `animationClass-add` and `animationClass-remove` classes to add animations:

```
@-webkit-keyframes ng-class-animation {
    from {
        background-color: white;
        color:black;
        border: 1px solid black;
    }

    to {
        background-color: black;
        color: white;
        border: 1px solid white;
    }
}

@keyframes ng-class-animation {
    from {
        background-color: white;
        color:black;
        border: 1px solid black;
    }

    to {
        background-color: black;
        color: white;
        border: 1px solid white;
    }
}
```

The initial state is shown as follows:

ngClass Animation

| Toggle ngClass |

This element has class 'initialClass' and the ngClass directive is declared as ng-class="{'animationClass' : toggleNgClass}"

So, we want to display an animation when `animationClass` is added to the element with the `initialClass` class by the `ngClass` directive. This way, our animation selector will be:

```
.initialClass.animationClass-add{
    -webkit-animation: 1s ng-class-animation;
    animation: 1s ng-class-animation;
}
```

After 500 ms, the result should be a complete gray `div` tag because the text, border, and background colors are halfway through the transition between black and white, as we can see in this screenshot:

After a second of animation, this is the result:

![ngClass Animation screenshot with Toggle ngClass button and black element containing text "This element has class 'initialClass' and the ngClass directive is declared as ng-class="{'animationClass' : toggleNgClass}""]

The remove animation, which occurs when `animationClass` is removed, is similar to the enter animation. However, this animation should be the reverse of the enter animation, and so, the CSS selector of the animation will be:

```
initialClass.animationClass-remove {
    -webkit-animation: 1s ng-class-animation reverse;
    animation: 1s ng-class-animation reverse;
}
```

The animation result will be the same as we saw in previous screenshots, but in the reverse order.

The ngHide and ngShow animation sample

Let's see one sample of the ngHide animation, which is the directive that shows and hides the given HTML code based on an expression, such as the ngShow directive. We will use this directive to create a success notification message that fades in and out.

To have a lean CSS file in this sample, we will use the Bootstrap CSS library, which is a great library to use with AngularJS. There is an AngularJS version of this library created by the Angular UI team available at http://angular-ui.github.io/bootstrap/.

The Twitter Bootstrap library is available at http://getbootstrap.com/.

For this sample, we will use the Microsoft CDN; you can check out the Microsoft CDN libraries at http://www.asp.net/ajax/cdn.

Consider the following HTML:

```
<!DOCTYPE html>
<html ng-app="myApp">
<head>
  <title>AngularJS ngHide sample</title>
</head>
<body>
  <link href="http://ajax.aspnetcdn.com/ajax/bootstrap/3.2.0/css/
    bootstrap.css" rel="stylesheet" />
  <style>
    /* ngHide animation */
    .ngHideSample {
      padding: 10px;
    }

      .ngHideSample.ng-hide-add {
        -webkit-transition: all linear 0.3s;
        -moz-transition: all linear 0.3s;
        -ms-transition: all linear 0.3s;
        -o-transition: all linear 0.3s;
        opacity: 1;
      }

      .ngHideSample.ng-hide-add-active {
        opacity: 0;
      }

      .ngHideSample.ng-hide-remove {
```

```
      -webkit-transition: all linear 0.3s;
      -moz-transition: all linear 0.3s;
      -ms-transition: all linear 0.3s;
      -o-transition: all linear 0.3s;
      opacity: 0;
    }

    .ngHideSample.ng-hide-remove-active {
      opacity: 1;
    }
  </style>
  <div>
    <h1>ngHide animation</h1>
    <div>
      <button ng-click="disabled = !disabled">Toggle ngHide
        animation</button>
      <div ng-hide="disabled" class="ngHideSample bg-success">
        This element has the ng-hide directive.
      </div>
    </div>
  </div>
  <script src="//ajax.googleapis.com/ajax/libs/angularjs
    /1.3.0/angular.min.js"></script>
  <script src="//ajax.googleapis.com/ajax/libs/angularjs
    /1.3.0/angular-animate.min.js"></script>
  <script>
    var app = angular.module('myApp', ['ngAnimate']);
  </script>
</body>
</html>
```

In this sample, we created an animation in which when the element is going to hide, its opacity is transitioned until it's set to 0. Also, when the element appears again, its opacity transitions back to 1 as we can see in the following sequence of screenshots.

In the initial state, the output is as follows:

After we click on the button, the notification message starts to fade:

ngHide animation

Toggle ngHide animation

This element has the ng-hide directive.

After the add (`ng-hide-add`) animation has completed, the output is as follows:

ngHide animation

Toggle ngHide animation

Then, if we toggle again, we will see the success message fading in:

ngHide animation

Toggle ngHide animation

This element has the ng-hide directive.

After the animation has completed, it returns to the initial state:

ngHide animation

Toggle ngHide animation

This element has the ng-hide directive.

The ngShow directive uses the same convention; the only difference is that each directive has the opposite behavior for the model value. When the model is true, ngShow removes the ng-hide class and ngHide adds the ng-hide class, as we saw in the first sample of this chapter.

The ngModel directive and form animations

We can easily animate form controls such as `input`, `select`, and `textarea` on `ngModel` changes. Form controls already work with validation CSS classes such as `ng-valid`, `ng-invalid`, `ng-dirty`, and `ng-pristine`. These classes are appended to form controls by AngularJS, based on validations and the current form control status. We are able to animate on the add and remove features of those classes.

So, let's see an example of how to change the input color to red when a field becomes invalid. This helps users to check for errors while filling in the form before it is submitted. The animation eases the validation error experience. For this sample, a valid input will contain only digits and will become invalid once a character is entered.

Consider the following HTML:

```
<h1>ngModel and form animation</h1>
<div>
  <form>
    <input ng-model="ngModelSample" ng-pattern="/^\d+$/"
class="inputSample" />
  </form>
</div>
```

This `ng-pattern` directive validates using the regular expression if the model `ngModelSample` is a number. So, if we want to warn the user when the input is invalid, we will set the input text color to red using a CSS transition.

Consider the following CSS:

```
/* ngModel animation */
.inputSample.ng-invalid-add {
    -webkit-transition: 1s linear all;
 transition: 1s linear all;
    color: black;
}

.inputSample.ng-invalid {
    color: red;
}

.inputSample.ng-invalid-add-active {
    color: red;
}
```

We followed the same pattern as `ngClass`. So, when the `ng-invalid` class is added, it will append the `ng-invalid-add` class and the transition will change the text color to red in a second; it will then continue to be red, as we have defined the `ng-invalid` color as `red` too. The test is easy; we just need to type in one non-numeric character on the input and it will display the animation.

The ngMessage and ngMessages directive animations

Both the `ngMessage` and `ngMessages` directives are complimentary, but you can choose which one you want to animate, or even animate both of them. They became separated from the core module, so we have to add the `ngMessages` module as a dependency of our AngularJS application.

These directives were added to AngularJS in Version 1.3, and they are useful to display messages based on the state of the model of a form control. So, we can easily display a custom message if an input has a specific validation error, for example, when the input is required but is not filled in yet. Without these directives, we would rely on JavaScript code and/or complex `ngIf` statements to accomplish the same result.

For this sample, we will create three different error messages for three different validations of a password field, as described in the following HTML:

```
<!DOCTYPE html>
<html ng-app="myApp">
<head>
  <title>ngMessages animation</title>
</head>
<body>
  <link href="ngMessageAnimation.css" rel="stylesheet" />
  <h1>ngMessage and ngMessages animation</h1>
  <div>
    <form name="messageAnimationForm">
      <label for="modelSample">Password validation input</label>
      <div>
        <input ng-model="ngModelSample" id="modelSample"
          name="modelSample" type="password" ng-pattern=
          "/^\d+$/" ng-minlength="5" ng-maxlength="10"
          required class="ngMessageSample" />
        <div ng-messages="messageAnimationForm.
          modelSample.$error" class="ngMessagesClass"
          ng-messages-multiple>
          <div ng-message="pattern" class="ngMessageClass">*
            This field is invalid, only numbers are allowed</div>
```

```
        <div ng-message="minlength" class="ngMessageClass">*
            It's mandatory at least 5 characters</div>
        <div ng-message="maxlength" class="ngMessageClass">*
            It's mandatory at most 10 characters</div>
      </div>
    </div>
  </form>
</div>
<script src="//ajax.googleapis.com/ajax/libs/angularjs
    /1.3.0/angular.min.js"></script>
<script src="//ajax.googleapis.com/ajax/libs/angularjs
    /1.3.0/angular-animate.min.js"></script>
<script src="//ajax.googleapis.com/ajax/libs/angularjs
    /1.3.0/angular-messages.min.js"></script>
<script>
  var app = angular.module('myApp', ['ngAnimate',
      'ngMessages']);
</script>
</body>
</html>
```

We included the ngMessage file too, as it's required for this sample.

For the ngMessages directive, that is, the container of the ngMessage directives, we included an animation on ng-active-add that changes the container background color from white to red and ng-inactive-add that does the opposite, changing the background color from red to white.

This works because the ngMessages directive appends the ng-active class when there is any message to be displayed. When there is no message, it appends the ng-inactive class to the element. Let's see the ngMessages animation's declaration:

```
.ngMessagesClass {
    height: 50px;
    width: 350px;
}

.ngMessagesClass.ng-active-add {
    transition: 0.3s linear all;
    background-color: red;
}

.ngMessagesClass.ng-active {
```

```
    background-color: red;
}

.ngMessagesClass.ng-inactive-add {
    transition: 0.3s linear all;
    background-color: white;
}

.ngMessagesClass.ng-inactive {
    background-color: white;
}
```

For the `ngMessage` directive, which contains a message, we created an animation that changes the color of the error message from transparent to white when the message enters the DOM, and changes the color from white to transparent when the message leaves DOM, shown as follows:

```
.ngMessageClass {
    color: white;
}

.ngMessageClass.ng-enter {
    transition: 0.3s linear all;
    color: transparent;
}

.ngMessageClass.ng-enter-active {
    color: white;
}

.ngMessageClass.ng-leave {
    transition: 0.3s linear all;
    color: white;
}

.ngMessageClass.ng-leave-active {
    color: transparent;
}
```

This sample illustrates two animations for two directives that are related to each other.

The initial result, before we add a password, is as follows:

We can see both animations being triggered when we type in the a character, for example, in the password input.

Between 0 and 300 ms of the animation, we will see both the background and text appearing for two validation messages:

After 300 ms, the animation has completed, and the output is as follows:

The ngView directive animation

The ngView directive is used to add a template to the main layout. It has support for animation, for both enter and leave events. It's nice to have an animation for ngView so the user has a better notion that we are switching views. For this directive sample, we need to add the ngRoute JavaScript file to the HTML and the ngRoute module as a dependency of our app.

We will create a sample that slides the content of the current view to the left, and the new view appears sliding from the right to the left too so that we can see the current view leaving and the next view appearing.

Consider the following HTML:

```
<!DOCTYPE html>
<html ng-app="myApp">
<head>
  <title>AngularJS ngView sample</title>
</head>
<body>
  <style>
    .ngViewRelative {
      position: relative;
      height: 300px;
    }

    .ngViewContainer {
      position: absolute;
      width: 500px;
      display: block;
    }

      .ngViewContainer.ng-enter,
      .ngViewContainer.ng-leave {
        -webkit-transition: 600ms linear all;
        transition: 600ms linear all;
      }

      .ngViewContainer.ng-enter {
        transform: translateX(500px);
      }

      .ngViewContainer.ng-enter-active {
```

```
        transform: translateX(0px);
      }


      .ngViewContainer.ng-leave {
        transform: translateX(0px);
      }


      .ngViewContainer.ng-leave-active {
        transform: translateX(-1000px);
      }
  </style>
  <h1>ngView sample</h1>
  <div class="ngViewRelative">
    <a href="#/First">First page</a>
    <a href="#/Second">Second page</a>
    <div ng-view class="ngViewContainer">
    </div>
  </div>
  <script src="//ajax.googleapis.com/ajax/libs/angularjs
    /1.3.0/angular.min.js"></script>
  <script src="//ajax.googleapis.com/ajax/libs/angularjs
    /1.3.0/angular-animate.min.js"></script>
  <script src="//ajax.googleapis.com/ajax/libs/angularjs
    /1.3.0/angular-route.min.js"></script>
  <script>
    var app = angular.module('myApp', ['ngAnimate', 'ngRoute']);
    app.config(['$routeProvider',
        function ($routeProvider) {
          $routeProvider
            .when('/First', {
              templateUrl: 'first.html'
            })
            .when('/Second', {
              templateUrl: 'second.html'
            })
            .otherwise({
              redirectTo: '/First'
            });

        }]);
  </script>
</body>
</html>
```

We need to configure the routes on `config`, as the JavaScript shows us. We then create two HTML templates on the same directory. The content of the templates are just plain lorem ipsum.

The `first.html` file content is shown as follows:

```
<div>
  <h2>First page</h2>
  <p>
    Lorem ipsum dolor sit amet, consectetur adipiscing elit.
      Cras consectetur dui nunc, vel feugiat lectus imperdiet et.
      In hac habitasse platea dictumst. In rutrum malesuada justo,
      sed porttitor dolor rutrum eu. Sed condimentum tempus est at
      euismod. Donec in faucibus urna. Fusce fermentum in mauris
      at pretium. Aenean ut orci nunc. Nulla id velit interdum
      nibh feugiat ultricies eu fermentum dolor. Pellentesque
      lobortis rhoncus nisi, imperdiet viverra leo ullamcorper
      sed. Donec condimentum tincidunt mollis. Curabitur lorem
      nibh, mattis non euismod quis, pharetra eu nibh.
  </p>
</div>
```

The `second.html` file content is shown as follows:

```
<div>
  <h2>Second page</h2>
  <p>
    Ut eu metus vel ipsum tristique fringilla. Proin hendrerit
      augue quis nisl pellentesque posuere. Aliquam sollicitudin
      ligula elit, sit amet placerat augue pulvinar eget. Aliquam
      bibendum pulvinar nisi, quis commodo lorem volutpat in.
      Donec et felis sit amet mauris venenatis feugiat non id
      metus. Fusce leo elit, egestas non turpis sed, tincidunt
      consequat tellus. Fusce quis auctor neque, a ultricies urna.
      Cras varius purus id sagittis luctus. Sed id lectus
      tristique, euismod ipsum ut, congue augue.
  </p>
</div>
```

Great, we now have our app set up to enable `ngView` and routes. The animation was defined by adding animation to the enter and leave events using `translateX()`.

This animation is defined to the new view coming from 500 px from the right and animating until the position on the x-axis is 0, leaving the view in the left corner. The leaving view goes from the initial position until it is at -1000 px on the x-axis. Then, it leaves the DOM. This animation creates a sliding effect; the leaving view leaves faster as it has to move double the distance of the entering view in the same animation duration.

We can change the translation using the y-axis to change the animation direction, creating the same sliding effect but with different aesthetics.

The ngSwitch directive animation

The ngSwitch directive is a directive that is used to conditionally swap the DOM structure based on an expression. It supports animation on the enter and leave events, for example, the ngView directive animation events.

For this sample, we will create the same sliding effect of the ngView sample, but in this case, we will create a sliding effect from top to bottom instead of right to left. This animation helps the user to understand that one item is being replaced by the other.

The ngSwitch sample HTML is shown as follows:

```
<!DOCTYPE html>
<html ng-app="myApp">
<head>
    <title>AngularJS ngSwitch sample</title>
</head>
<body>
    <div ng-controller="animationsCtrl">
        <h1>ngSwitch sample</h1>
        <p>Choose an item:</p>
        <select ng-model="ngSwitchSelected" ng-options="item for item
in ngSwitchItems"></select>
        <p>Selected item:</p>
        <div class="switchItemRelative" ng-switch
          on="ngSwitchSelected">
            <div class="switchItem" ng-switch-when="item1">Item
              1</div>
            <div class="switchItem" ng-switch-when="item2">Item
              2</div>
            <div class="switchItem" ng-switch-when="item3">Item
              3</div>
            <div class="switchItem" ng-switch-default>Default
              Item</div>
        </div>
    </div>
    <script src="//ajax.googleapis.com/ajax/libs/angularjs
      /1.3.0/angular.min.js"></script>
    <script src="//ajax.googleapis.com/ajax/libs/angularjs
      /1.3.0/angular-animate.min.js"></script>
    <script>
```

```
            var app = angular.module('myApp', ['ngAnimate']);
            app.controller('animationsCtrl', function ($scope) {
                $scope.ngSwitchItems = ['item1', 'item2', 'item3'];
            });
        </script>
    </body>
</html>
```

In the JavaScript controller, we added the `ngSwitchItems` array to the scope, and the animation CSS is defined as follows:

```
/* ngSwitch animation */
.switchItemRelative {
    position: relative;
    height: 25px;
    overflow: hidden;
}

.switchItem {
    position: absolute;
    width: 500px;
    display: block;
}
/*The transition is added when the switch item is about to
  enter or about to leave DOM*/
.switchItem.ng-enter,
.switchItem.ng-leave {
    -webkit-transition: 300ms linear all;
    -moz-transition: 300ms linear all;
    -ms-transition: 300ms linear all;
    -o-transition: 300ms linear all;
    transition: 300ms linear all;
}

/* When the element is about to enter DOM*/
.switchItem.ng-enter {
    bottom: 100%;
}

/* When the element completes the enter transition */
.switchItem.ng-enter-active {
    bottom: 0;
}
/* When the element is about to leave DOM*/
.switchItem.ng-leave {
```

```
    bottom: 0;
}
/*When the element end the leave transition*/
.switchItem.ng-leave-active {
    bottom: -100%;
}
```

This is almost the same CSS as the ngView sample; we just used the bottom property, added a different height to the switchItemRelative class, and included overflow:hidden.

The ngInclude directive sample

The ngInclude directive is used to fetch, compile, and include an HTML fragment; it supports animations for the enter and leave events, such as the ngView and ngSwitch directives. For this sample, we will use both templates created in the last ngView sample, first.html and second.html.

The ngInclude animation sample HTML with JavaScript and CSS included is shown as follows:

```
<!DOCTYPE html>
<html ng-app="myApp">
<head>
  <title>AngularJS ngInclude sample</title>
</head>
<body>
  <style>
    .ngIncludeRelative {
      position: relative;
      height: 500px;
      overflow: hidden;
    }

    .ngIncludeItem {
      position: absolute;
      width: 500px;
      display: block;
    }

      .ngIncludeItem.ng-enter,
      .ngIncludeItem.ng-leave {
        -webkit-transition: 300ms linear all;
```

```
      transition: 300ms linear all;
    }

    .ngIncludeItem.ng-enter {
      top: 100%;
    }

    .ngIncludeItem.ng-enter-active {
      top: 0;
    }

    .ngIncludeItem.ng-leave {
      top: 0;
    }

    .ngIncludeItem.ng-leave-active {
      top: -100%;
    }
  </style>
  <div ng-controller="animationsCtrl">
    <h1>ngInclude sample</h1>
    <p>Choose one template</p>
    <select ng-model="ngIncludeSelected" ng-options="item.name for
      item in ngIncludeTemplates"></select>
    <p>ngInclude:</p>
    <div class="ngIncludeRelative">
      <div class="ngIncludeItem" ng-
        include="ngIncludeSelected.url"></div>
    </div>
  </div>
  <script src="//ajax.googleapis.com/ajax/libs/angularjs
    /1.3.0/angular.min.js"></script>
  <script src="//ajax.googleapis.com/ajax/libs/angularjs
    /1.3.0/angular-animate.min.js"></script>
  <script>
    var app = angular.module('myApp', ['ngAnimate']);
    app.controller('animationsCtrl', function ($scope) {
      $scope.ngIncludeTemplates = [{ name: 'first', url:
        'first.html' }, { name: 'second', url: 'second.html' }];
    })
  </script>
</body>
</html>
```

In the JavaScript controller, we included the templates array.

Finally, we can animate `ngInclude` using CSS. In this sample, we will animate by sliding the templates using the `top` property, using the enter and leave events animation. To test this sample, just change the template value selected.

Do it yourself exercises

The following are some exercises that you can refer to that will help you understand the concepts of this chapter better:

1. Create a spinning loading animation using the `ngShow` or `ngHide` directives that appears when the scope controller variable, `$scope.isLoading`, is equal to `true`.

2. Using exercise 1, create a gray background layer with opacity 0.5 that smoothly fills the entire page behind the loading spin, and after page content is loaded, covers all the content until `isProcessing` becomes `false`. The effect should be that of a drop of ink that is dropped on a piece of paper and spreads until it's completely stained.

3. Create a success notification animation, similar to the `ngShow` example, but instead of using the fade animation, use a slide-down animation. So, the success message starts with `height:0px`. Check `http://api.jquery.com/slidedown/` for the expected animation effect.

4. Copy any animation from the `http://capptivate.co/` website, using AngularJS and CSS animations.

Summary

In this chapter, we learned how to animate AngularJS native directives using the CSS transitions and CSS keyframe concepts that we learned in the previous chapter. This chapter taught you how to create animations on AngularJS web apps.

Now we are capable of creating the most common animations. We had a good introduction to how AngularJS `ngAnimate` fits together with CSS animations, and we are now prepared to know how to create AngularJS animations using JavaScript, which we will learn in the next chapter.

4
JavaScript Animations in AngularJS

We have already learned how to create animations using CSS in the context of AngularJS. Now we will learn how to create animations using JavaScript in AngularJS.

In this chapter, we will learn the following topics:

- Creating AngularJS animations without CSS3
- The `ngHide` directive JavaScript animation
- The `ngIf` directive JavaScript animation
- The `ngRepeat` directive JavaScript animation
- JavaScript animations as fallback for CSS animations

Creating AngularJS animation without CSS3

The AngularJS animation module enables us to create animations with CSS3 or JavaScript. Now we will learn how to animate an AngularJS directive using purely JavaScript so that we can create animations even for browsers without support of CSS3, or integrate with some commonly used JavaScript animations libraries such as jQuery animate and GSAP JS.

For this chapter, we will use jQuery as the JavaScript animations library because it's very intuitive and well known. We will integrate this library with AngularJS native directives so that we can easily get the built-in benefits of AngularJS and animate using jQuery. The documentation can be found at `http://api.jquery.com/animate/`.

First, we have to declare the animation using the `animation()` method; the declaration is really similar to the way in which you define an AngularJS factory. We specify the class of target elements where we want to display the animation on the first parameter of the animation method. The `ngAnimate` module of AngularJS checks whether there is any animation defined for the DOM manipulation event that is being triggered. It also checks for transitions, animations, and JavaScript animation callback functions. If at least one of these exists, it triggers the animations.

For the JavaScript animations declaration, we define callback functions to be called when an element with the same class as defined on the animation method triggers an event like `addClass`. If there is a callback defined for this `addClass` event, it's called; otherwise, it skips the animation step.

Check the following animation sample for the `ngClass` directive. In this sample, we will create a button that closes an info message using the `slideUp` effect from jQuery and opens the info message using the `slideDown` effect from jQuery, shown as follows:

```
/**
 * @name firstJsAnimation
 * @desc The first sample animation function
 */
function firstJsAnimation() {

    /**
     * @name addClassAnimation
     * @desc The animation function called when a class is removed
         from the element
     * @param element - The element that will have the class
         removed
     * @param className - The name of the class that will be
         removed from the element
     * @param done - Callback function, it must be called to
         finish the animation
     */
    var addClassAnimation = function (element, className, done) {
        //Check if the class added is the one that triggers
          the animation
        if (className != 'animationClass') {
            return;
        }

        //Animate to slide up and then call done function
```

```
        jQuery(element).slideUp(300, done);

        // Here is the optional return function that treats
          completed or cancelled animations
        return function (isCancelled) {
            if (isCancelled) {
                element.stop();
            }
        };
}


/**
* @name removeClassAnimation
* @desc The animation function called when a class is
  removed from the element
* @param element - The element that will have the
  class removed
* @param className - The name of the class that will be
  removed from the element
* @param done - Callback function, it must be called to
  finish the animation
*/
var removeClassAnimation = function (element,
  className, done) {
    //Check if the class removed is the one that
      triggers the animation
    if (className != 'animationClass') {
        return;
    }

    //Animate to slide down and then call done function
    jQuery(element).slideDown(300, done);


    // Here is the optional return function that
      treats completed or cancelled animations
    return function (isCancelled) {
        if (isCancelled) {
            element.stop();
        }
    };
}

return {
    addClass: addClassAnimation,
```

```
                removeClass: removeClassAnimation
        };

    }

    var app = angular.module('myApp', ['ngAnimate'])
        .animation(".firstJsAnimation", firstJsAnimation);
```

We defined two animation callback functions for directives with the
firstJsAnimation class.

Here is the HTML in which we included the bootstrap CSS just to add information
style for the animation div:

```
<!DOCTYPE html>
<html ng-app="myApp">
<head>
  <title>AngularJS JavaScript animations - ngClass</title>
</head>
<body>
  <link href="http://ajax.aspnetcdn.com/ajax/bootstrap
    /3.2.0/css/bootstrap.css" rel="stylesheet" />
  <h2>ngClass JavaScript Animation</h2>
  <button ng-click="toggleNgClass = !toggleNgClass">
    Toggle ngClass animation</button>
  <div ng-class="{'animationClass' : toggleNgClass}"
    class="firstJsAnimation alert alert-info">
    This element has class 'ngClassAnimationSample' and
      the ngClass directive is declared as
      ng-class="{'animationClass' : toggleNgClass}"
  </div>
  <script src="//ajax.googleapis.com/ajax/libs/jquery/1.11.1
    /jquery.min.js"></script>
  <script src="//ajax.googleapis.com/ajax/libs/angularjs
    /1.3.0/angular.min.js"></script>
  <script src="//ajax.googleapis.com/ajax/libs/angularjs
    /1.3.0/angular-animate.min.js"></script>
  <script src="jsAnimationNgClass.js"></script>
</body>
</html>
```

When we click on the **Toggle ngClass** animation button, animationClass is added
to the element with the firstJsAnimation class, so the ngAnimate module will
check if there is an addClass animation callback function for elements with the
firstJsAnimation class. If there is any, it will trigger the animation by calling the
callback function.

AngularJS JavaScript animation works on the principle of callback functions. Each callback function has at least two parameters: `element`, which is the DOM element to be animated, and `done`, which is a callback function used to tell AngularJS when the animations are completed by calling it. We have passed the `done` function to jQuery's animate callback parameter in the sample; it's mandatory to call this function so that the `$animate` service knows when the animation is completed.

Each callback function can return an optional function that is called when the animation is completed or the execution has been canceled. We can tell whether the animation has been canceled or executed by the first parameter that is a Boolean; if that is `true`, it means that the animation has been cancelled and if it is `false`, it means the animation has been executed. In our samples, we added a treatment for cancelled animations, stopping the element jQuery animation. This might happen, for example, if you click twice on the **Toggle ngClass animation** button before the first animation has completed.

Let's see what happens on the last `ngClass` sample using JavaScript for the slide animation. The last sample starts with:

ngClass JavaScript Animation

Toggle ngClass animation

This element has class 'ngClassAnimationSample' and the ngClass directive is declared as ng-class="{'animationClass' : toggleNgClass}"

After we click on the **Toggle ngClass animation** button, it starts to slide up, shown as follows:

ngClass JavaScript Animation

Toggle ngClass animation

This element has class 'ngClassAnimationSample' and the ngClass directive is declared as ng-class="{'animationClass' : toggleNgClass}"

After the animation is completed, it vanishes, shown as follows:

ngClass JavaScript Animation

Toggle ngClass animation

The animate module expects the return of an object with at least one of the following callback functions defined. The events that can be defined in this object are `enter`, `leave`, `move`, `beforeAddClass`, `addClass`, `beforeRemoveClass`, and `removeClass`. They are the same events that trigger CSS animations, so for each animation directive, you should create the relative animation callback functions.

Each callback function has its proper signature, so you should follow this:

```
function enter(element, done){
  return function finish(isCancelled){} }
function leave(element, done){
  return function finish(isCancelled){} }
function move(element, done){
  return function finish(isCancelled){} }
function beforeAddClass(element, className, done){
  return function finish(isCancelled){} }
function addClass(element, className, done){
  return function finish(isCancelled){} }
function beforeRemoveClass(element, className, done){
  return function finish(isCancelled){} }
function removeClass(element, className, done){
  return function finish(isCancelled){} }
```

The first parameter is always the DOM element.

The `className` class name is passed to the `beforeAddClass`, `addClass`, `removeClass`, and `beforeRemoveClass` callback functions, so in these functions, you know if the class added or removed is the one you want to animate or some other class for the same element.

The `beforeAddClass` callback function is called before the class is added, and the `addClass` function is called after the class is added. The same for `beforeRemoveClass` that is called before the class is removed and `removeClass` is called after the class is removed.

The convention here is similar to the CSS naming convention, and the table of directives and events supported from the previous chapter are the same; it's just different the way we define the animation. Refer to the following table:

Directive	Supported animations	Function
ngRepeat	Enter, leave, and move	`function(element, done) { return function finish(isCancelled){} }`
ngView	Enter and leave	`function(element, done) { return function finish(isCancelled){} }`
ngInclude	Enter and leave	`function(element, done) { return function finish(isCancelled){} }`
ngSwitch	Enter and leave	`function(element, done) { return function finish(isCancelled){} }`
ngIf	Enter and leave	`function(element, done) { return function finish(isCancelled){} }`
ngClass	Add and remove	`function (element, className, done){ return function finish(isCancelled) {} }`
ngShow and ngHide	Add and remove	`function (element, className, done){ return function finish(isCancelled) {} }`
form and ngModel	Add and remove	`function (element, className, done){ return function finish(isCancelled) {} }`
ngMessages	Add and remove	`function (element, className, done){ return function finish(isCancelled) {} }`
ngMessage	Enter and leave	`function(element, done) { return function finish(isCancelled){} }`

The preceding table shows us the native directives with the respective supported animations and the callback function signature of each animation event.

The ngHide JavaScript animation

Let's see another sample of JavaScript animation with the ngHide native directive. As we saw in the previous table, the ngHide directive has two animation events (the add and remove classes). So, our JavaScript animation should have two callback functions, beforeAddClass and removeClass.

We use the beforeAddClass callback function because when the ng-hide class is added, the display:none; style is applied. The removeClass callback function is used instead of the beforeRemoveClass callback function because the display:none; style is still applied.

Consider the following animation definition:

```
/**
 * @name hideJsAnimation
 * @desc The ngHide sample animation function
 */
function hideJsAnimation() {
    function animateOpacity(element, done, opacity) {
        jQuery(element).animate({
            opacity: opacity,
            height: ["toggle", "swing"]
        }, 3000, done);
    }

    /**
     * @name beforeAddClassAnimation
     * @desc The animation function called before a class is added to
the element
     * @param element - The element that will have the class appended
     * @param className - The name of the class that will be appended
to the element
     * @param done - Callback function, it must be called to finish the
animation
     */
    var beforeAddClassAnimation = function (element, className, done)
{
        //Animate the opacity and style the height to display a
curtain effect
        animateOpacity(element, done, 0);

        // Here is the optional return function that treats completed
or cancelled animations
        return function (isCancelled) {
            if (isCancelled) {
```

```
                element.stop();
            }
        };
    }
    /**
     * @name removeClassAnimation
     * @desc The animation function called when a class is removed from
the element
     * @param element - The element that will have the class removed
     * @param className - The name of the class that will be removed
from the element
     * @param done - Callback function, it must be called to finish the
animation
     */
    var removeClassAnimation = function (element, className, done) {
        animateOpacity(element, done, 1);

        // Here is the optional return function that treats completed
or cancelled animations
        return function (isCancelled) {
            if (isCancelled) {
                element.stop();
            }
        };
    }

    return {
        beforeAddClass: beforeAddClassAnimation,
        removeClass: removeClassAnimation
    };

}


var app = angular.module('myApp', ['ngAnimate'])
    .animation(".hideJsAnimation", hideJsAnimation);
```

This animation used jQuery's animate swing effect to apply a certain effect to the element. In this sample, we didn't check whether the `className` parameter is ng-hide because in this sample, there won't be any other class being added or removed from this element. However, it's recommended to add a check function to check whether it's really the class added or removed that we are expecting to trigger the animation, just like we did in the other sample.

Consider the following HTML code:

```
<!DOCTYPE html>
<html ng-app="myApp">
<head>
  <title>AngularJS JavaScript animations - ngHide</title>
</head>
<body>
  <div>
    <h2>ngHide Animation</h2>
    <button ng-click="hide = !hide">Hide/Show the div below</button>
    <div ng-hide="hide" class="hideJsAnimation">
      This is a div element with ng-hide="hide"
    </div>
  </div>
  <script src="//ajax.googleapis.com/ajax/libs/jquery/1.11.1/jquery.
min.js"></script>
  <script src="//ajax.googleapis.com/ajax/libs/angularjs/1.3.0/
angular.min.js"></script>
  <script src="//ajax.googleapis.com/ajax/libs/angularjs/1.3.0/
angular-animate.min.js"></script>
  <script src="jsAnimationNgHide.js"></script>
</body>
</html>
```

The HTML has just a simple button that toggles the hide variable that will trigger the ng-hide directive on the div element with the hideJsAnimation class.

The ngIf JavaScript animation

Now, we will see a sample of the ngIf JavaScript animation. As listed in the table where we have discussed about directives and supported animations, we know that this directive supports animations in the enter and leave events.

So, we will create a fade effect similar to the ngHide sample; the difference is in the events that each directive triggers.

Consider the following JavaScript animation declaration:

```
/**
 * @name ifJsAnimation
 * @desc The ngIf sample animation function
 */
function ifJsAnimation() {
    function animateOpacity(element, done, opacity) {
```

```
            jQuery(element).animate({
                opacity: opacity
            }, 3000, done);
        }


    /**
     * @name enterAnimation
     * @desc The enter animation function called when an element enters
DOM
     * @param element - The element that is entering DOM
     * @param done - Callback function, it must be called to finish the
animation
     */
    var enterAnimation = function (element, done) {
        //Animate the opacity
        jQuery(element).css({ opacity: 0 });
        animateOpacity(element, done, 1);


        // Here is the optional return function that treats completed
or cancelled animations
        return function (isCancelled) {
            if (isCancelled) {
                element.stop();
            }
        };
    }


    /**
     * @name leaveAnimation
     * @desc The leave animation function called when an element leaves
DOM
     * @param element - The element that is leaving DOM
     * @param done - Callback function, it must be called to finish the
animation
     */
    var leaveAnimation = function (element, done) {
        animateOpacity(element, done, 0);


        // Here is the optional return function that treats completed
or cancelled animations
        return function (isCancelled) {
            if (isCancelled) {
                element.stop();
            }
        };
```

```
    }

    return {
        enter: enterAnimation,
        leave: leaveAnimation
    };

}

var app = angular.module('myApp', ['ngAnimate'])
    .animation(".ifJsAnimation", ifJsAnimation);
```

As we can see, it's almost the same; the only difference is that we don't have the `className` parameter as the element enters or leaves DOM during the events.

Consider the following HTML that uses `ngIf`:

```html
<!DOCTYPE html>
<html ng-app="myApp">
<head>
  <title>AngularJS JavaScript animations - ngIf</title>
</head>
<body>
  <div>
     <h2>ngIf Animation</h2>
     <button ng-click="toggling = !toggleNgIf">Display/Remove the div
below</button>
     <div ng-if="toggling" class="ifJsAnimation">
       This is a div element with ng-if="toggling"
     </div>
  </div>
  <script src="//ajax.googleapis.com/ajax/libs/jquery/1.11.1/jquery.
min.js"></script>
  <script src="//ajax.googleapis.com/ajax/libs/angularjs/1.3.0/
angular.min.js"></script>
  <script src="//ajax.googleapis.com/ajax/libs/angularjs/1.3.0/
angular-animate.min.js"></script>
  <script src="jsAnimationNgIf.js"></script>
</body>
</html>
```

The HTML is very straightforward; there is a button that changes the value of the `toggling` variable and the `div` element using the `ngIf` directive and the `toggling` variable with the `ifJsAnimation` class.

The ngRepeat JavaScript animation

We have already learned how the enter, leave, addClass, and removeClass events can be handled by JavaScript animations. Let's see how we can animate the move event, which is used only by the ngRepeat directive.

Consider the following HTML with the ngRepeat directive and a Sort button similar to the ngRepeat CSS animation sample:

```
<!DOCTYPE html>
<html ng-app="myApp">
<head>
  <title>AngularJS JavaScript animations - ngRepeat</title>
</head>
<body>
  <div ng-controller="repeatController as rc">
    <h2>ngRepeat Animation</h2>
    <button ng-click="rc.sortItems()">Sort items</button>
    <div ng-repeat="item in rc.items" class="repeatItemAnimation">
      {{item.name}}
    </div>
  </div>
  <script src="//ajax.googleapis.com/ajax/libs/jquery/1.11.1/jquery.
min.js"></script>
  <script src="//ajax.googleapis.com/ajax/libs/angularjs/1.3.0/
angular.min.js"></script>
  <script src="//ajax.googleapis.com/ajax/libs/angularjs/1.3.0/
angular-animate.min.js"></script>
  <script src="jsAnimations.js"></script>
</body>
</html>
```

The JavaScript with the controller and animation is as follows:

```
/**
 * @name repeatControllerFn
 * @desc Repeat sample controller
 */
function repeatControllerFn() {
    var rc = this;
    rc.items = [{ name: 'David' }, { name: 'Adailton' }, { name:
'Claudio' }, { name: 'Cleomar' }, { name: 'Filipe' }];

    /**
     * @name sortItems
     * @desc Sort items array
```

```
    */
    rc.sortItems = function () {
        rc.items.sort(function (a, b) { return a[name] < b[name] ? -1
: 1 });
    };
}


/**
 * @name repeatItemAnimation
 * @desc The ngRepeat sample animation function
 */
function repeatItemAnimation() {
    /**
     * @name moveAnimation
     * @desc The move animation function called when an element moves
in DOM
     * @param element - The element that is moving in DOM
     * @param done - Callback function, it must be called to finish the
animation
     */
    var moveAnimation = function (element, done) {
        jQuery(element).css({ opacity: 0 });
        jQuery(element).animate({
            opacity: 1
        }, 3000, done);

        // Here is the optional return function that treats completed
or cancelled animations
        return function (isCancelled) {
            if (isCancelled) {
                element.stop();
            }
        };
    }

    return {
        move: moveAnimation
    };
}


var app = angular.module('javascriptSample', ['ngAnimate'])
    .controller("repeatController", repeatControllerFn)
    .animation(".repeatItemAnimation", repeatItemAnimation);
```

The move callback function signature is the same as the enter and leave callback functions. We used the same animation as used on the leave event of the ngIf directive sample. When we click on the **Sort Items** button, the elements are sorted, and so, it triggers the ngRepeat animation for the moved elements.

JavaScript animations as a fallback for CSS animations

We might have to create animations for browsers that do not have support for CSS animations and transitions yet. It might be part of a project's requirements.

In this case, we can still use JavaScript animations as a fallback for CSS animations. However, what if we add a CSS animation and a JavaScript animation for the same element and the browser has support for CSS animations?

We don't want to display the same animation twice, so we will use **Modernizr**, a JavaScript library that detects HTML5 and CSS3 features in the user's browser.

 Learn more about Modernizr at http://modernizr.com.

In such cases, we will trigger the JavaScript animations only if CSS transitions are not supported by the browser.

Here, we have a sample of the ngIf animation that uses a transition if the browser has support for CSS transitions; otherwise, it triggers the JavaScript animation fallback with the same animation effect, shown as follows:

```
<!DOCTYPE html>
<html ng-app="myApp">
<head>
  <title>AngularJS JavaScript animations - ngIf</title>
</head>
<body>
  <style>
    /* ngIf animation */
    .ifJsAnimation.ng-enter,
    .ifJsAnimation.ng-leave {
      -webkit-transition: opacity ease-in-out 1s;
```

```
        transition: opacity ease-in-out 1s;
    }

    .ifJsAnimation.ng-enter,
    .ifJsAnimation.ng-leave.ng-leave-active {
      opacity: 0;
    }

    .ifJsAnimation.ng-leave,
    .ifJsAnimation.ng-enter.ng-enter-active {
      opacity: 1;
    }
  </style>

  <div>
    <h2>ngIf with CSS Animation and fallback for JavaScript
animation</h2>
    <button ng-click="toggleNgIf = !toggleNgIf">Display/Remove the div
below</button>
    <div ng-if="toggleNgIf" class="ifJsAnimation">
      This is a div element with ng-if="toggleNgIf"
    </div>
  </div>
  <script src="//ajax.googleapis.com/ajax/libs/jquery/1.11.1/jquery.
min.js"></script>
  <script src="//ajax.googleapis.com/ajax/libs/angularjs/1.3.0/
angular.min.js"></script>
  <script src="//ajax.googleapis.com/ajax/libs/angularjs/1.3.0/
angular-animate.min.js"></script>
  <script src="modernizr.js"></script>
  <script src="jsAnimationNgIfFallback.js"></script>
</body>
</html>
```

The JavaScript will remain the same as that from the ngIf sample, but we will check
whether the browser has support for CSS transitions, shown as follows:

```
/**
 * @name ifJsAnimation
 * @desc The ngIf sample animation function
 */
function ifJsAnimation() {
    function animateOpacity(element, done, opacity) {
        jQuery(element).animate({
            opacity: opacity
```

```
    }, 1000, done);
  }


  /**
  * @name enterAnimation
  * @desc The enter animation function called when an element enters
DOM
  * @param element - The element that is entering DOM
  * @param done - Callback function, it must be called to finish the
animation
  */
  var enterAnimation = function (element, done) {

      if (!Modernizr.csstransitions) {
          //Animate the opacity
          jQuery(element).css({ opacity: 0 });
          animateOpacity(element, done, 1);

          // Here is the optional return function that treats
completed or cancelled animations
          return function (isCancelled) {
              if (isCancelled) {
                  element.stop();
              }
          };
      } else {
          done();
      }
  }


  /**
  * @name leaveAnimation
  * @desc The leave animation function called when an element leaves
DOM
  * @param element - The element that is leaving DOM
  * @param done - Callback function, it must be called to finish the
animation
  */
  var leaveAnimation = function (element, done) {
      if (!Modernizr.csstransitions) {
          animateOpacity(element, done, 0);

          // Here is the optional return function that treats
completed or cancelled animations
          return function (isCancelled) {
```

```
                    if (isCancelled) {
                        element.stop();
                    }
                };
            }
            else {
                done();
            }
        }

        return {
            enter: enterAnimation,
            leave: leaveAnimation
        };

    }

    var app = angular.module('myApp', ['ngAnimate'])
        .animation(".ifJsAnimation", ifJsAnimation);
```

If you want to test this sample and only have modern browsers installed, you can test using Internet Explorer 11. It has a simulator for older IE browsers in the developer tools; try with IE9 for this sample.

The same strategy works for CSS keyframe animations, but we should check using the Modernizr.cssanimations property.

Do it yourself exercises

The following are some exercises that will help you understand the concept of this chapter better:

1. Create a fade-in/fade-out animation using CSS animation, but create a fallback for CSS transition in case CSS animation is not supported, and then create a JavaScript fallback if both CSS animation and CSS transitions are not supported. Tip: use Modernizr.

2. Create a single JavaScript animation for AngularJS using jQuery and apply the single animation for more than one element.

Summary

In this chapter, we learned how to animate AngularJS native directives using JavaScript animations and how similar it is to the CSS convention. We created JavaScript animation samples using jQuery animate.

Now we are capable of creating the most common animations using CSS or JavaScript. There is something still missing; how can we integrate AngularJS with custom directives? This is the topic of the next chapter.

Custom Directives and the $animate Service

5

We already learned how to create animations using both JavaScript and CSS in the AngularJS context for native directives. Now, we will learn how to animate custom directives and how to use the `$animate` service.

In this chapter, we will learn the following topics:

- Triggering animations on custom directives
- Animating the `enter` and `leave` events
- Using the `$animate.move` method
- Creating a custom directive animation with JavaScript

Triggering animations on custom directives

Now that we already know how to create animations for native directives, it would be nice if we could add animations to custom directives too. Sometimes, we might want to add motion to custom directives, think about a responsive menu directive that hides the menu when it's on a small device, and have a button to open or slide the menu items. An animation triggered inside this directive would be great.

This is accomplished by injecting the `$animate` service into the directive function. This is the same service used by native directives to trigger the animation events we learned in *Chapter 3, Creating Our First Animation in AngularJS*, and *Chapter 4, JavaScript Animations in AngularJS*.

In the custom directive, we can trigger events by calling `$animate` methods such as `enter`, `leave`, `move`, `addClass`, `removeClass`, and `setClass`.

Here, we will see a sample of the `addClass` and `removeClass` animations on a custom directive, which are the same events used by the ngClass, ngHide and ngShow, and ngMessages native directives.

To create our first custom directive animation, we need to know the `$animate` method's signatures:

```
$animate.addClass(element, className);
$animate.removeClass(element, className);
```

Both functions receive the `element` parameter that will have a class added or removed and the `className` class that will be used and return a promise that is resolved once the animation has completed itself or has been cancelled. This is different from just appending and removing a class from the element by jQuery, because the `$animate` service checks whether there is any animation for the element and triggers the animation.

Check this basic directive that triggers the animation events by adding and removing the `customClick` class when the `$element` service is clicked:

```
var app = angular.module('myApp', ['ngAnimate'])
.directive('customDirective', function ($animate) {
    return {
        link: function ($scope, $element, $attrs) {
            var isActive = true;
            $element.on('click', function () {
                isActive = !isActive;
                // Toggle between add class and remove class
                if (isActive) {
                    $animate.addClass($element, 'customClick');
                } else {
                    $animate.removeClass($element,
                        'customClick');
                }
                //Trigger digest in this case, because this
listener function is out of the angular world
                $scope.$apply();
            });
        }
    });
```

Here is the HTML code:

```html
<!DOCTYPE html>
<html ng-app="myApp">
<head>
  <title>AngularJS Custom Directives animations</title>
  <link href="custom.css" rel="stylesheet" />
</head>
<body>
  <h1>AngularJS Custom Directives animations</h1>
  <div custom-directive class="customAnimation">
    <p>This element has class 'customAnimation' and the directive
      attribute "custom-directive"</p>
    <p>Click here to toggle animation</p>
  </div>
  <script src="//ajax.googleapis.com/ajax/libs/angularjs/1.3.0
    /angular.min.js"></script>
  <script src="//ajax.googleapis.com/ajax/libs/angularjs/1.3.0
    /angular-animate.min.js"></script>
  <script src="customDirective.js"></script>
</body>
</html>
```

We will use the same animation as was used in the ngClass sample:

```css
.customAnimation {
    background-color: blue;
    padding: 20px;
    transition: all linear 1s;
}

.customClick {
    background-color: yellow;
    padding: 40px;
}

.customAnimation.customClick-add {
    animation: 1s ng-class-animation;
}

@keyframes ng-class-animation {
    from {
        background-color: white;
```

```
        border: 1px solid black;
    }

    to {
        background-color: black;
        border: 1px solid white;
    }
}
```

The $animate.addClass method adds the className class to the element. It follows the same steps as triggered by the ngClass directive.

1. $animate.addClass(element, 'className') is called by the directive.
2. If there is any JavaScript animation defined for the element, the $animate service runs the JavaScript animation.
3. The .className-add class is added to the element.
4. The $animate service waits for a single animation frame, which causes a page reflow.
5. Both the .className and .className-add-active classes are added to the element, triggering the CSS transitions and animations.
6. The $animate service scans the element styles to get the CSS transitions and/or animations duration and delay.
7. The $animate service waits until the animation is completed.
8. The animation ends and all generated CSS classes are removed from the element but the .className class is kept on the element.
9. The returned promise is resolved.

This is a step-by-step procedure that occurs on native and custom directives that uses $animate.addClass as the ngClass and our custom directive directives.

The steps from the $animate.removeClass method are similar:

1. $animate.removeClass(element, 'className') is called by the directive.
2. If there is any JavaScript animation defined for the element, the $animate service runs the JavaScript animation.
3. The .className-remove class is added to the element.
4. The $animate service waits for a single animation frame, which causes a page reflow.
5. The .className-remove-active class is added to the element, and the class .className is removed triggering the CSS transitions and/or animations.

6. The $animate service scans the element styles to get the CSS transitions or animations duration and delay.

7. The $animate service waits until the animation is completed.

8. The animation ends and all generated CSS classes are removed from the element.

9. The returned promise is resolved.

In this section, we learned how to use $animate.addClass and $animate.removeClass. There are three more methods that can be used to trigger animations:

```
$animate.enter(element, parentElement, afterElement);
$animation.leave(element);
$animation.move(element, parentElement, afterElement);
```

Animating the enter and leave events

The methods used to trigger the enter and leave animation events from the $animate service are $animate.enter and $animate.leave. They are the same animation events triggered by the ngIf, ngInclude, ngView, ngSwitch, ngRepeat, and ngMessage directives when an element is entered or removed from DOM.

The $animate.enter method adds the element sibling to the afterElement node or appends to the parentElement parameter and then runs the enter animation. After the animation is finished, the returned promise is resolved.

The method signature is as follows:

```
$animate.enter(element, parentElement, afterElement)
```

The enter method follows these steps:

1. $animate.enter(element, parentElement, afterElement) is called by the directive.

2. The element is inserted in parentElement or sibling to afterElement if the parentElement is not defined.

3. $animate waits for the next digest to start the animation.

4. If there is any JavaScript animation defined for the element, the $animate service runs the JavaScript animation.

5. The .ng-enter class is added to the element.

6. The $animate service scans the element styles to get the CSS transitions or animations duration and delay.

7. $animate blocks all CSS transitions on the element, so the .ng-enter class is affected immediately.

8. The $animate service waits for a single animation frame, and this causes a page reflow.

9. $animate unblocks the CSS transitions from the element.

10. The .ng-enter-active class is added to the element, triggering the CSS transitions and animations.

11. The $animate service waits until the animation is completed.

12. The animation ends and all generated CSS classes are removed from the element.

13. The returned promise is resolved.

The $animate.leave method executes the leave animation and then removes the element from DOM. If the doneCallback is defined, call this function after the animation is finished.

The $animate.leave method signature is as follows:

```
$animate.leave(element)
```

The leave method follows these steps:

1. $animate.leave(element) is called by the directive.

2. If there is any JavaScript animation defined for the element, the $animate service runs the JavaScript animation.

3. $animate waits for the next digest to start the animation.

4. The .ng-leave class is added to the element.

5. The $animate service scans the element styles to get the duration of and delay in CSS transitions or animations.

6. $animate blocks all CSS transitions on the element, so the .ng-leave class is affected immediately.

7. The $animate service waits for a single animation frame. This causes a page reflow.

8. $animate unblocks the CSS transitions from the element.

9. The .ng-leave-active class is added to the element triggering the CSS transitions and animations.

10. The $animate service waits until the animation is completed.

11. The animation ends, and all generated CSS classes are removed from the element.

12. The element is removed from DOM.

13. The returned promise is resolved.

To illustrate the use of both methods, we will create a directive named `toggleDirective` that toggles two elements. So, on every click, while one element enters, the other one leaves.

The `toggleDirective` sample directive code that uses the `enter` and `leave` events is as follows:

```
var app = angular.module('myApp', ['ngAnimate'])
.directive('toggleDirective', function ($animate) {
    return {
        link: function ($scope, $element, $attrs) {
            var firstElement = angular.element('<div
                class="toggleAnimation">First element! Click here
to trigger $animate.leave for this element and $animate.enter for the
second element</div>');
            var secondElement = angular.element('<div
                class="toggleAnimation">Second element! Click
                here to trigger $animate.leave for this
                element and $animate.enter for the first
                element</div>');

            //Adds the firstElement
            $animate.enter(firstElement, $element);

            var isActive = false;

            $element.on('click', function () {
                isActive = !isActive;
                // Toggle between firstElement and secondElement
                if (isActive) {
                    $animate.leave(firstElement);
                    $animate.enter(secondElement, $element);
                } else {
                    $animate.leave(secondElement);
                    $animate.enter(firstElement, $element);
                }
                //Trigger digest in this case, because this
listener function is out of the angular world
                $scope.$apply();
            });
```

```
            }
        }

    });
```

The HTML code that uses `toggleDirective` is as follows:

```
<!DOCTYPE html>
<html ng-app="myApp">
<head>
  <title>AngularJS Custom Directives animations</title>
  <link href="custom.css" rel="stylesheet" />
</head>
<body>
  <h2>Toggle using enter and leave</h2>
  <div toggle-directive="" class="enterAnimation"></div>
  <script src="//ajax.googleapis.com/ajax/libs/angularjs/1.3.0/
angular.min.js"></script>
  <script src="//ajax.googleapis.com/ajax/libs/angularjs/1.3.0/
angular-animate.min.js"></script>
  <script src="toggleDirective.js"></script>
</body>
</html>
```

The animation CSS that will be used by this sample is as follows:

```
/* toggle animation */
.toggleAnimation.ng-enter,
.toggleAnimation.ng-leave {
    -webkit-transition: opacity ease-in-out 1s;
    transition: opacity ease-in-out 1s;
}

.toggleAnimation.ng-enter,
.toggleAnimation.ng-leave.ng-leave-active {
    opacity: 0;
}

.toggleAnimation.ng-leave,
.toggleAnimation.ng-enter.ng-enter-active {
    opacity: 1;
}
```

This sample shows a simple use case where we add one element to DOM and remove another element. The same animation can be defined in JavaScript too. The same method called by our custom directive is called from the native directives, so the animation definition is the same in both cases.

Using the $animate.move method

The method that moves one element from one place to another in DOM and triggers animation is `$animate.move`. It's used by the ngRepeat directive, and it can be used in any custom directive that moves DOM elements too.

The signature is the same as the `$animate.enter` method; the only difference is that the element is not added to DOM, but it's moved:

```
$animate.move(element, parentElement, afterElement);
```

The steps are similar to the `$animate.enter` method:

1. `$animate.move(element, parentElement, afterElement)` is called by the directive.
2. The element is moved in `parentElement` or a sibling to `afterElement` if `parentElement` is not defined.
3. `$animate` waits for the next digest to start the animation.
4. If there is any JavaScript animation defined for the element, the `$animate` service runs the JavaScript animation.
5. The `.ng-move` class is added to the element.
6. The `$animate` service scans the element styles to get the duration of and delay in CSS transitions or animations.
7. `$animate` blocks all CSS transitions on the element, so the `.ng-move` class is affected immediately.
8. The `$animate` service waits for a single animation frame, and this causes a page reflow.
9. `$animate` unblocks the CSS transitions from the element.
10. The `.ng-move-active` class is added to the element, triggering the CSS transitions and animations.
11. The `$animate` service waits until the animation is completed.
12. The animation ends and all generated CSS classes are removed from the element.
13. The returned promise is resolved.

For this sample, we will create a directive with three elements and move these elements on click.

The HTML code for the `moveDirective` custom directive is as follows:

```
<!DOCTYPE html>
<html ng-app="myApp">
<head>
  <title>AngularJS Custom Directives animations</title>
  <link href="custom.css" rel="stylesheet" />
</head>
<body>
  <h2>$animate move sample</h2>
  <p>Click on any element below to move elements:</p>
  <div move-directive="">
    <div class="element1 moveItem">Element 1</div>
    <div class="element2 moveItem">Element 2</div>
    <div class="element3 moveItem">Element 3</div>
  </div>
  <script src="//ajax.googleapis.com/ajax/libs/angularjs/1.3.0/
angular.min.js"></script>
  <script src="//ajax.googleapis.com/ajax/libs/angularjs/1.3.0/
angular-animate.min.js"></script>
  <script src="moveDirective.js"></script>
</body>
</html>
```

The `moveDirective` directive will move the last element to the top on each click:

```
var app = angular.module('myApp', ['ngAnimate'])
    .directive('moveDirective', function ($animate) {
        return {
            link: function ($scope, $element, $attrs) {
                var elements = $element.children();
                var count = 0;

                $element.on('click', function () {
                    count++;
                    // Toggle between firstElement and secondElement
                    if (count % 3 == 1) {
                        $animate.move(angular.element(elements[2]),
$element);
                    } else if (count % 3 == 2) {
                        $animate.move(angular.element(elements[1]),
$element);
                    } else {
```

```
                    $animate.move(angular.element(elements[0]),
$element);
                }
                //Trigger digest in this case, because this
listener function is out of the angular world
                $scope.$apply();
            });
        }
      }

    });
```

We will use the same CSS animation as was used in the ngRepeat move sample in *Chapter 3, Creating Our First Animation in AngularJS*:

```
.moveItem.ng-move {
    -webkit-animation: 1s ng-move-repeat-animation;
    animation: 1s ng-move-repeat-animation;
}
```

This sample shows us how to animate elements from a custom directive by triggering the move animation.

Creating a custom directive animated with JavaScript

We already learned how to create CSS animations for custom directives. What if we still want to use JavaScript animations for those directives?

Remember the ngIf JavaScript animation from *Chapter 4, JavaScript Animations in AngularJS*? We can reuse that JavaScript animation here. We will keep using the same JavaScript declaration method that we learned in *Chapter 4, JavaScript Animations in AngularJS*.

For this sample, we will create a directive similar to the toggleDirective sample using the enter and leave animation methods. Check the HTML code of the following sample without any CSS:

```
<!DOCTYPE html>
<html ng-app="myApp">
<head>
   <title>AngularJS Custom Directives animations</title>
</head>
```

```
<body>
  <h1>AngularJS Custom Directives animations</h1>
  <div toggle-Js-class-directive="" class="ifJsAnimation">
  </div>
  <script src="//ajax.googleapis.com/ajax/libs/jquery/1.11.1/jquery.
min.js"></script>
  <script src="//ajax.googleapis.com/ajax/libs/angularjs/1.3.0/
angular.min.js"></script>
  <script src="//ajax.googleapis.com/ajax/libs/angularjs/1.3.0/
angular-animate.min.js"></script>
  <script src="toggleJsDirective.js"></script>
</body>
</html>
```

Now, we will use the same JavaScript animation declaration from the ngIf JavaScript animation sample. Our directive will use the $animate.enter and $animate.leave methods to the enter and leave elements with the ifJsAnimation class from DOM, and this is where the animation will be hooked; check the following JavaScript:

```
/**
 * @name ifJsAnimation
 * @desc The ngIf sample animation function
 */
function ifJsAnimation() {
    function animateOpacity(element, done, opacity) {
        jQuery(element).animate({
            opacity: opacity
        }, 3000, done);
    }

    /**
     * @name enterAnimation
     * @desc The enter animation function called when an element enters
DOM
     * @param element - The element that is entering DOM
     * @param done - Callback function, it must be called to finish the
animation
     */
    var enterAnimation = function (element, done) {
        //Animate the opacity
        jQuery(element).css({ opacity: 0 });
        animateOpacity(element, done, 1);

        // Here is the optional return function that treats completed
or cancelled animations
```

```
            return function (isCancelled) {
                if (isCancelled) {
                    element.stop();
                }
            };
        }


        /**
         * @name leaveAnimation
         * @desc The leave animation function called when an element leaves
DOM
         * @param element - The element that is leaving DOM
         * @param done - Callback function, it must be called to finish the
animation
         */
        var leaveAnimation = function (element, done) {
            animateOpacity(element, done, 0);


            // Here is the optional return function that treats completed
or cancelled animations
            return function (isCancelled) {
                if (isCancelled) {
                    element.stop();
                }
            };
        }


        return {
            enter: enterAnimation,
            leave: leaveAnimation
        };


}

function toggleClassFn($animate) {
    return {
        link: function ($scope, $element, $attrs) {
            var isActive = false;
            var firstElement = angular.element('<div
class="ifJsAnimation">First element! Click here to trigger $animate.
leave for this element and $animate.enter for the second element</
div>');
```

```
            var secondElement = angular.element('<div
class="ifJsAnimation">Second element! Click here to trigger $animate.
leave for this element and $animate.enter for the first element</
div>');

                //Adds the firstElement
                $animate.enter(firstElement, $element);

                $element.on('click', function () {
                    isActive = !isActive;
                    // Toggle between firstElement and secondElement
                    if (isActive) {
                        $animate.leave(firstElement);
                        $animate.enter(secondElement, $element);
                    } else {
                        $animate.leave(secondElement);
                        $animate.enter(firstElement, $element);
                    }
                    //Trigger digest in this case, because this listener
function is out of the angular world
                    $scope.$apply();
                });
            }
        }
    }

var app = angular.module('myApp', ['ngAnimate'])
    .directive('toggleJsClassDirective', toggleClassFn)
    .animation('.ifJsAnimation', ifJsAnimation);
```

At this point, we already saw how flexible the Angular ngAnimate module is and how reusable our animation's declarations are. We are even able to create a CSS animation definition with a fallback for the JavaScript animation and reuse it in native and custom directives.

Exercises

1. Create a "hamburger" menu, a commonly used menu in mobile apps with three lines on a button, which when clicked, slides the menu items from the left or top. Use the $animate service to hook animations in the enter and leave events.

2. Create an animation using CSS animations with a fallback for the JavaScript animation. Apply this single animation in both native and custom directives.

3. Create a card custom directive, similar to a Google+ post, or similar to a Windows 8 tile, that contains a button to flip it, to see the cover of the card. Create the flip animation using CSS animations.

4. Create a magazine page directive, which when clicked on the page, opens the following page by flipping the current page to the left. This is similar to Steller animations (`http://steller.co/`).

Summary

In this chapter, we learned how to animate AngularJS custom directives and how to use the `$animate` service.

We learned what happens inside the native AngularJS directives and how to use the same animation events on any custom directive.

Now, we are able to create animations in any directive using CSS or JavaScript. The next chapter will explain how to use animations and enhance the usability on small devices such as smartphones.

6
Animations for Mobile Devices

We already learned how to create animations using both JavaScript and CSS in the AngularJS context for native and custom directives. Now, we will learn how to enhance the user experience of our AngularJS web app, especially on mobile devices and tablets.

In this chapter, we will learn the following topics:

- Enhance the UX on mobile devices with animations
- Transition between views
- Mobile AngularJS frameworks

Enhance UX on mobile devices with animations

With the increasing use of smartphones and tablet devices, more people have started to visit websites via smartphones and other devices, so not optimizing a web app for small devices is not an option anymore.

Nowadays, we create a single web app that is responsive to the device width using **CSS3 media queries**. So, we are able to define different styles for each device width size. We can provide a better experience based on the screen size.

Currently, web apps are run on small screens of devices such as smartphones and also on screens as big as that of TVs. It's impossible to create a CSS style for each device width in the world, so usually, we work with different ranges of screen widths: smartphones, tablets and small desktops, and big desktops monitors.

As we usually use CSS animations to animate in the AngularJS context, we are able to define animations in a specific media query. So, we might disable some heavy-processing animations and enable other GPU-accelerated animations for small screens. We will learn more about GPU-accelerated animations in *Chapter 8, Animations' Performance Optimization*.

To learn more about media query, check out `https://developer.mozilla.org/en-US/docs/Web/Guide/CSS/Media_queries`.

A recently launched design guideline from Google, called **material design** (visit `http://www.google.com/design`) helps us enhance the UX of our web apps on mobile devices and desktops too.

The motion created by animations on web apps is better delivered when it seems more realistic. One of the material design guidelines is to avoid linear animations as it's a more mechanical and artificial movement than animations with acceleration and deceleration at the beginning and ending of an animation curve. This guideline is called **authentic motion**. Another important guideline is **meaningful transitions**, the next section's subject.

Transition between views

The Google material design website explains transitioning as follows:

> *"Transitioning between two visual states should be smooth, appear effortless, and above all, provide clarity to the user, not confusion. A well-designed transition does the heavy lifting and enables the user to clearly understand where their attention should be focused. A transition has three categories of elements."*

The three categories of elements are the incoming elements, outgoing elements, and shared elements.

A common transition to web apps is changing the main content view, for instance, using `ngView` or `ngInclude`. Smartphones and devices with touchscreens provide a different interaction for the user. Taps and gestures are used instead of clicks. The ngTouch module enables us to use swipe gestures and the ngClick directive is replaced for a better tap experience on touchscreen devices.

For this transition, we will create an animation of pages (the incoming element) sliding from the right to the left over another page (the outgoing element) by a swipe-to-left gesture; the leave page will slide to the same direction.

The followings pages, except the last one, have the swipe-to-right and swipe-to-left gesture listeners, so the user can go forward or go back to pages and the slide animation follows the use swipe direction. This is a common approach in mobile apps user interaction. Currently, the Facebook app has a similar behavior.

When we swipe the second page to the right (the outgoing element), the first page enters sliding it from the left to the right as the second page is sliding in the same direction.

The following screenshot sequence shows the swipe-to-left gesture animation effect:

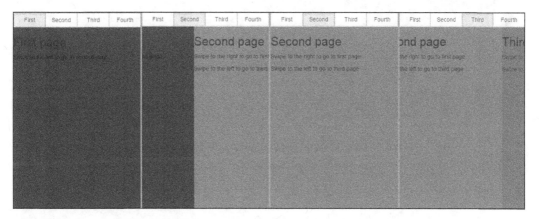

As we saw in the last sequence of screenshots, we swiped from the right to the left and users still could click on the tab buttons on the top if they didn't want to swipe.

The next sequence shows what happens when we keep swiping to the left. Pages keep sliding from the right to the left:

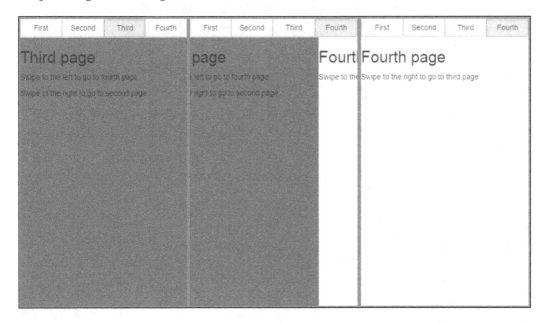

Now, we will swipe to the right once, and then, we will click on the **First** button to open the first page. The following screenshot sequence shows the effect:

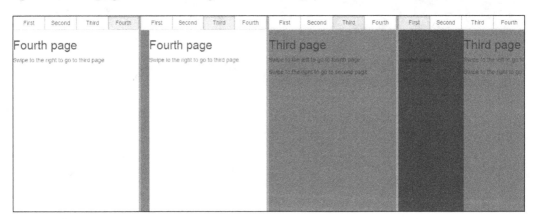

Finally, in the first page shown in the following screenshot, the animation direction follows the tab bar order. It's much more intuitive than views sliding from the right to the left:

To create this transition of views animation, we will use the ngInclude directive and a source code similar to our ngInclude sample from *Chapter 3, Creating Our First Animation in AngularJS*.

The HTML code is as follows; we included the Bootstrap CSS only to use the top buttons style:

```
<!DOCTYPE html>
<html ng-app="myApp">
<head>
  <title>AngularJS Swipe Slider animation</title>
  <meta name="viewport" content="width=device-width,height=device-
height,user-scalable=no">
```

```html
    <link href="mobile.css" rel="stylesheet" />
    <link href="http://ajax.aspnetcdn.com/ajax/bootstrap/3.2.0/css/
bootstrap.css" rel="stylesheet" />
  </head>
  <body>
    <div ng-controller="tabsSwipeCtrl as responsive">
      <div class="btn-group btn-group-justified">
        <div class="btn-group">
          <button type="button" class="btn btn-default" ng-
click="responsive.selectPage(0)" ng-class="{'active': responsive.
ngIncludeSelected.index == 0}">First</button>
        </div>
        <div class="btn-group">
          <button type="button" class="btn btn-default" ng-
click="responsive.selectPage(1)" ng-class="{'active': responsive.
ngIncludeSelected.index == 1}">Second</button>
        </div>
        <div class="btn-group">
          <button type="button" class="btn btn-default" ng-
click="responsive.selectPage(2)" ng-class="{'active': responsive.
ngIncludeSelected.index == 2}">Third</button>
        </div>
        <div class="btn-group">
          <button type="button" class="btn btn-default" ng-
click="responsive.selectPage(3)" ng-class="{'active': responsive.
ngIncludeSelected.index == 3}">Fourth</button>
        </div>
      </div>
      <div class="ngIncludeRelative">
        <div class="ngIncludeItem" ng-include="responsive.
ngIncludeSelected.url" ng-class="{'moveToLeft' : responsive.
moveToLeft}"></div>
      </div>
    </div>
    <script src="//ajax.googleapis.com/ajax/libs/angularjs/1.3.0/
angular.min.js"></script>
    <script src="//ajax.googleapis.com/ajax/libs/angularjs/1.3.0/
angular-touch.min.js"></script>
    <script src="//ajax.googleapis.com/ajax/libs/angularjs/1.3.0/
angular-animate.min.js"></script>
    <script src="tabsSwipeCtrl.js"></script>
  </body>
</html>
```

We added the `ngSwipeLeft` and `ngSwipeRight` directives from the ngTouch module to the partial view, so the user can change between views by swiping gestures.

The `firstSwipe.html` partial view is as follows:

```
<div class="firstPage page" ng-swipe-left="responsive.selectPage(1)">
  <h2>First page</h2>
  <p>Swipe to the left to go to second page</p>
</div>
```

The `secondSwipe.html` partial view is as follows:

```
<div class="secondPage page" ng-swipe-left="responsive.selectPage(2)"
ng-swipe-right="responsive.selectPage(0)">
  <h2>Second page</h2>
  <p>Swipe to the right to go to first page</p>
  <p>Swipe to the left to go to third page</p>
</div>
```

The `thirdSwipe.html` partial view is as follows:

```
<div class="thirdPage page" ng-swipe-left="responsive.selectPage(3)"
ng-swipe-right="responsive.selectPage(1)">
  <h2>Third page</h2>
  <p>Swipe to the left to go to fourth page</p>
  <p>Swipe to the right to go to second page</p>
</div>
```

The `fourthSwipe.html` partial view is as follows:

```
<div class="page" ng-swipe-right="responsive.selectPage(2)">
  <h2>Fourth page</h2>
  <p>Swipe to the right to go to third page</p>
</div>
```

To create the desired animation effect, we will use a combination of `ngInclude` and `ngClass`. The ngClass directive will be used to learn the direction of the animation on the enter and leave events of the pages.

We will define the controller in the `tabsSwipeCtrl.js` file:

```
function tabsSwipeCtrlFn() {
    var responsive = this;
    responsive.ngIncludeTemplates = [{ index: 0, name: 'first', url:
'firstSwipe.html' }, { index: 1, name: 'second', url: 'secondSwipe.
html' }, { index: 2, name: 'third', url: 'thirdSwipe.html' }, { index:
3, name: 'fourth', url: 'fourthSwipe.html' }];
```

```
        responsive.selectPage = selectPage;


        /**
         * Initialize with the first page opened
         */
        responsive.ngIncludeSelected =
            responsive.ngIncludeTemplates[0];


        /**
         * @name selectPage
         * @desc The function that includes the page of the indexSelected
         * @param indexSelected the index of the page to be included
         */
        function selectPage(indexSelected) {
            if (responsive.ngIncludeTemplates[indexSelected].index >
                responsive.ngIncludeSelected.index) {
                responsive.moveToLeft = false;
            } else {
                responsive.moveToLeft = true;
            }
            responsive.ngIncludeSelected =
                responsive.ngIncludeTemplates[indexSelected];
        }
    }


    var app = angular.module('myApp', ['ngAnimate', 'ngTouch'])
        .controller('tabsSwipeCtrl', tabsSwipeCtrlFn);
```

This combination of the moveToLeft, ng-enter, and ng-leave classes are used to trigger the animations in the mobile.css file using the direction based on the current page and the tab page the user will navigate to:

```
/* To avoid a horizontal scrollbar when the page enters/leaves the
view */
body {
    overflow-x: hidden;
}


.ngIncludeItem {
    position: absolute;
    top: 35px;
    bottom: 0;
    right: 0;
    left: 0;
    animation-duration: 0.30s;
```

```
    animation-timing-function: ease-in-out;
}

.page {
    position: inherit;
    top: 0;
    right: inherit;
    bottom: inherit;
    left: inherit;
}

.firstPage {
    background-color: blue;
}

.secondPage {
    background-color: red;
}

.thirdPage {
    background-color: green;
}

/* When the page enters, slide it from the right */
.ngIncludeItem.ng-enter {
    animation-name: slideFromRight;
    -webkit-animation-name: slideFromRight;
}
/* When the page enters and moveToLeft is true, slide it from the
left(out of the user view) to the right (left corner) */
.ngIncludeItem.moveToLeft.ng-enter {
    animation-name: slideFromLeft;
    -webkit-animation-name: slideFromLeft;
}
/* When the page leaves, slide it to left(out of the user view) from
the left corner,
    in other words slide it from the left(out of the view) to the left
corner but in reverse order */
.ngIncludeItem.ng-leave {
    animation-name: slideFromLeft;
    animation-direction: reverse;
    -webkit-animation-name: slideFromLeft;
    -webkit-animation-direction: reverse;
}
```

```
/* When the page leaves, slide it to the right(out of the user view)
from the the left corner,
    in other words, slide it from the right but in reverse order  */
.ngIncludeItem.moveToLeft.ng-leave {
    animation-name: slideFromRight;
    animation-direction: reverse;
    -webkit-animation-name: slideFromRight;
    -webkit-animation-direction: reverse;
}

@keyframes slideFromRight {
    0% {
        transform: translateX(100%);
    }

    100% {
        transform: translateX(0);
    }
}

@keyframes slideFromLeft {
    0% {
        transform: translateX(-100%);
    }

    100% {
        transform: translateX(0);
    }
}
```

We saw a good sample of how to get a more native app feeling to the user using pure AngularJS animations with native directives.

AngularJS 2.0 Touch Animations is currently being drafted, and its focus is to provide better solutions for mobile devices, the same focus as that of AngularJS 2.0. This draft includes better handling of scrolling through a list using a finger, circling through pictures in a carousel, removing of items on swipe, and more native app features.

We can expect improvements for the future on AngularJS core, so things such as the infinite scrolling core will be standardized and not spread to many third-party AngularJS modules, as it's on the time this book is been written.

Mobile AngularJS frameworks

Nowadays, mobile features can be added to AngularJS web apps using external frameworks such as Ionic (see `http://ionicframework.com/`). It provides some great directives that uses the ngAnimate module behind the scenes to create those touch animations features.

The Ionic framework is a framework for hybrid mobile apps with HTML5. In other words, the framework is focused on the use of native apps, not for responsive web apps. This is a good choice if you want to create native apps using HTML, CSS, and JavaScript together with Apache Cordova or PhoneGap.

To learn more about Cordova, check out `http://cordova.apache.org/`.

To know more about PhoneGap, see `http://phonegap.com/`.

Another framework for mobile development built on top of AngularJS is the Mobile Angular UI. For more information, visit `http://mobileangularui.com/`.

Summary

In this chapter, we learned how to use animations with AngularJS to provide a better experience for responsive web apps, especially on small devices such as smartphones and tablets. We were introduced to the material design guideline and how to implement better animations and enhance the use of AngularJS web apps on mobile devices. We got a preview of what would come natively in the future of AngularJS too.

In the next chapter, we will learn about staggering animations.

7
Staggering Animations

A staggering animation is a group of animations that are triggered with a small delay between each successive operation. It's an often desirable animation and AngularJS 1.3 has support for these animations natively.

In this chapter, we will learn the following topics:

- Creating staggering animations
- Creating staggering animations for other native directives
- Adding staggering animations for custom directives

Creating staggering animations

Staggering animations provides a curtain effect; each animation starts with a small delay from the start of the last animation and before the last animation finishes.

Staggering animations are very useful to support the information hierarchy, as it creates a path for the eyes to follow, and it's useful to keep a consistent motion choreography so that the user doesn't get disoriented. Imagine a photo gallery website that might load all photos and show all of them at once or append the photos in a sequence, so the user don't get a lot of information at the same time.

Both points are explained in the *Meaningful Transitions* section of Google Material Design. Learn more about it at `http://www.google.com/design/spec/animation/meaningful-transitions.html`.

AngularJS has native support for these animations. It's as easy to create as declaring a `.ng-EVENT-stagger` CSS definition. This will apply the delay between animations for the `EVENT` animation, the EVENT being one of the animation events such as `enter`, `leave`, `add`, `remove`, and `move`.

The .ng-EVENT-stagger class has to define the transition-delay or animation-delay property. The first property is for transition animations and the second for keyframes animations.

Staggering animations with a CSS transition

We will create a staggering animation sample for the ngRepeat directive to understand it better. We will use filters on the repeaters so that we can remove and add back elements easily just by changing the input values with the filter's models. We will reuse the same stagger animations with the ngIf directive too:

```
<!DOCTYPE html>
<html ng-app="myApp">
<head>
  <title>AngularJS Staggering animations</title>
  <link href="http://ajax.aspnetcdn.com/ajax/bootstrap
    /3.2.0/css/bootstrap.css" rel="stylesheet" />
  <link href="staggered.css" rel="stylesheet" />
</head>
<body>
  <div ng-controller="staggeredCtrl as stagger">
    <h1>ngRepeat Transition staggering sample</h1>
    <button ng-click="showEmailsTransitions =
      !showEmailsTransitions">Show/Hide email list</button>
    <button ng-click="stagger.archive()">Archive AngularJS
      emails</button>
    <label for="filterBy">Filter email by:</label>
    <input ng-model="stagger.filterBy" name="filterBy" />
    <div ng-repeat="item in stagger.emails |
      filter:stagger.filterBy" ng-if="showEmailsTransitions"
      class="repeatItemTransition bg-primary">
      {{item}}
    </div>
    <h1>ngRepeat Animation staggering sample</h1>
    <button ng-click="showEmails = !showEmails">Show/Hide email
      list</button>
    <button ng-click="stagger.archive()">Archive AngularJS
      emails</button>
    <label for="animationFilterBy">Filter items by:</label>
    <input ng-model="stagger.animationFilterBy"
      name="animationFilterBy" />
    <div ng-repeat="item in stagger.emails |
      filter:stagger.animationFilterBy" ng-if="showEmails"
      class="repeatItem bg-primary">
      {{item}}
```

```
        </div>
    </div>
    <script src="//ajax.googleapis.com/ajax/libs/angularjs/1.3.0
      /angular.min.js"></script>
    <script src="//ajax.googleapis.com/ajax/libs/angularjs/1.3.0
      /angular-animate.min.js"></script>
    <script src="staggeredCtrl.js"></script>
</body>
</html>
```

In this HTML code, we used the ngRepeat directive twice for the same item's model just to learn how to stagger animations using transitions or keyframes animations.

The transition animation is described by the CSS fragment of the staggered.css file:

```
/* ngRepeat animation*/
.repeatItemTransition.ng-enter,
.repeatItemTransition.ng-leave {
    -webkit-transition: opacity ease-in-out 1s;
    transition: opacity ease-in-out 1s;
}

.repeatItemTransition.ng-enter,
.repeatItemTransition.ng-leave.ng-leave-active {
    opacity: 0;
}

.repeatItemTransition.ng-leave,
.repeatItemTransition.ng-enter.ng-enter-active {
    opacity: 1;
}

.repeatItemTransition.ng-enter-stagger,
.repeatItemTransition.ng-leave-stagger {
    /* This is the delay between each animation of the staggered
animation sequence */
    -webkit-transition-delay: 0.1s;
    transition-delay: 0.1s;

    /* This should be set to 0s to avoid problems, this element could
inherit the value from the repeatItemTransition element */
    -webkit-transition-duration: 0s;
    transition-duration: 0s;
}
```

The `ng-enter` and `ng-leave` classes usage is already well known in this chapter of the book. The only new detail in this sample is that to create staggering animations, we use the `.ng-enter-stagger` and `.ng-leave-stagger` classes on the same element with the `.repeatItemTransition` class.

These classes are where we should declare the delay time between the animations to be staggered, using the `transition-delay` property. Notice that we must set the duration of this animation to `0s`, using the `transition-duration` property, just to avoid the undesirable CSS inheritance that can remove the stagger effect.

The `staggeredCtrl.js` content is as follows:

```
function staggeredCtrlFn() {
    var stagger = this;
    stagger.emails = ["AngularJS news", "AngularJS rocks!", "AngularJS
animations", "Packt Publishing news", "AngularJS Jobs"];
    stagger.archive = archiveFn;

    function archiveFn() {
        stagger.emails = ["Packt Publishing news"];
    }
}
angular.module('myApp', ['ngAnimate'])
    .controller('staggeredCtrl', staggeredCtrlFn);
```

The controller scope just contains an array of e-mail items to be displayed with the ngRepeat directive and a dumb archive function that removes the e-mail items related to AngularJS.

Initially, we will get the following screenshot result:

When we click on the **Show/Hide email list** button of the transition sample, we will change the value of the ngIf directive expression. It will then trigger the enter animation with a curtain effect, as we can see in the next screenshot:

Finally, after the last animation is completed, we will have the following result:

In this sample, if we set p in the filter input that uses `filterBy`, we will see each of the e-mails that doesn't contain "p" in the text disappearing gracefully one after the other, as the leave animations will be staggered. This transition gives time for the user to understand which e-mails are being filtered from the view. The next screenshot displays the leave animations in different transition steps for each item:

The same leave staggered effect is displayed if we click on the **Archive AngularJS emails** button when there is no filter set, as the only e-mail left would be **Packt Publishing news**. The user will see which e-mails are being removed.

Staggering animations with a CSS keyframes animation

In the last sample template, the second ngRepeat directive doesn't have the .repeatItemTransition class, but it contains the .repeatItem class. So, to create a staggering animation with a similar effect of the last sample using keyframes animation, we should declare the following CSS:

```
.repeatItem.ng-enter-stagger,
.repeatItem.ng-leave-stagger{
    /* This is the delay between each animation of the staggered
animation sequence, now for keyframes animations */
    -webkit-animation-delay: 0.2s;
    animation-delay: 0.2s;

    /* This should be set to 0s to avoid problems too, this element
could inherit the value from the repeatItem element */
    -webkit-animation-duration: 0;
    animation-duration: 0;
}
```

This is the CSS fragment that defines the staggered animation delay. It's almost the same as the transition sample, we just exchanged the `transition-delay` property for `animation-delay` and `transition-duration` for `animation-duration`; both properties are used for the same purpose as the first element to set the delay between animations and avoid an inheritance that can break the staggering effect.

For this sample, we will use the same animation used in *Chapter 3*, *Creating Our First Animation in AngularJS*, in the ngRepeat directive sample; so the CSS fragment needed is:

```css
.repeatItem.ng-enter {
    -webkit-animation: 1s ng-enter-repeat-animation;
    animation: 1s ng-enter-repeat-animation;
}

.repeatItem.ng-leave {
    -webkit-animation: 1s ng-leave-repeat-animation;
    animation: 1s ng-leave-repeat-animation;
}
```

If we set "p" in the filter input named `animationFilterBy`, we will see each of the items that doesn't contain "p" in the text disappearing gracefully one after the other, as the next screenshot displays:

Creating staggering animations for other native directives

Alright, now we know how to create the staggering effect using the `ngRepeat` and `ngIf` directives in the `enter` and `leave` animation events; but, how to create staggering effects for other directives?

First, we need to understand how staggering happens. Angular enqueues the animations for elements with the **same parent element**, the **same animation event**, and the **same CSS classes**, and the animations should be triggered in less than 10 ms of each animation to be staggered. Otherwise, they will be considered as separated animations that should not be queued in the same sequence, and this doesn't mean that the delay should be less than 10 ms.

You might think that this happens only when we use `ngRepeat`, but it's not true. To prove it might apply for other directives too, let's create an `ngClass` staggering animation sample with the preceding rule in mind.

It's hard to figure out how to apply different staggering animations if we have all these restrictions to apply the stagger effect. We will show how to do it by using the `:nth-child()` CSS3 pseudo-class.

Check out the following HTML code, we have created two `div` elements with the same classes and the ngClass directive, below the same common parent of the ID, `parentElement`:

```
<!DOCTYPE html>
<html ng-app="myApp">
<head>
  <title>AngularJS Staggering animations</title>
  <link href="staggered.css" rel="stylesheet" />
</head>
<body>
  <h1>ngClass Staggering animation </h1>
  <div id="parentElement">
    <button ng-click="toggleNgClass = !toggleNgClass">Toggle ngClass
animation</button>
    <div ng-class="{'animationClass' : toggleNgClass}"
class="ngClassAnimationSample">
      First element
    </div>
    <div ng-class="{'animationClass' : toggleNgClass}"
class="ngClassAnimationSample">
      Second element
    </div>
```

```
  </div>
  <script src="//ajax.googleapis.com/ajax/libs/angularjs/1.3.0/
angular.min.js"></script>
  <script src="//ajax.googleapis.com/ajax/libs/angularjs/1.3.0/
angular-animate.min.js"></script>
  <script>
    angular.module('myApp', ['ngAnimate']);
  </script>
</body>
</html>
```

The ngClass directive will add the `animationClass` class to each element when the `toggleNgClass` variable becomes `true`.

The initial state is represented in the following screenshot:

When we click on the **Toggle ngClass animation** button for the first time, it will change the `toggleNgClass` variable to `true`. So, the two `div` elements with the `ngClassAnimationSample` class of the same `div` parent element of the `parentElement` ID will simultaneously trigger the add class animations. So, if we define the `animationClass-add-stagger` class besides the animation classes CSS, we will have the staggering effect for this animation. The big difference in this sample is that we will use two different definitions of `.animationClass-add-active` for each element even though they have the same CSS. We will use the `#parentElement>div:nth-child(2n+1).animationClass-add-active` selector, so all even `div` elements that are children of the element with the `parentElement` ID will have a different active class. So, the animation result will be different for the first and second elements:

```
/* ngclass animation */
.ngClassAnimationSample {
    background-color: white;
    border: 1px solid black;
}


.ngClassAnimationSample.animationClass-add-stagger {
```

```
        -webkit-transition-delay: 0.3s;
        transition-delay: 0.3s;
        -webkit-transition-duration: 0;
        transition-duration: 0;
}


.ngClassAnimationSample.animationClass-add {
        -webkit-transition: all ease-in-out 1s;
        transition: all ease-in-out 1s;
}


.ngClassAnimationSample.animationClass-add-active {
        background-color: black;
}


#parentElement>div:nth-child(2n+1).animationClass-add-active  {
        background-color: red;
}
```

Following the rule described in this topic, we can figure out many ways to create staggering animations with native directives and animation events.

The result after clicking on the **Toggle ngClass animation** button is as follows:

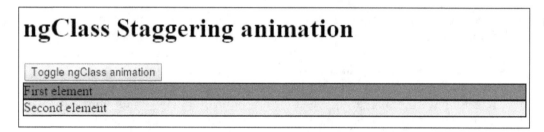

We can see that the first element gets darker before the second element becomes red.

Create staggering animations for custom directives

Alright, now we know how to create the staggering effect using native directives. What about creating staggering effects for custom directives?

We must keep this in mind: AngularJS enqueues the animations for the same parent element, the same classes, and the same animation event, and the animations should be triggered between 0 ms and 10 ms to be staggered. This has already been explained in the last topic, but this is important and deserves a reminder.

This is what happened in the first sample; the ngRepeat called $animate.enter and $animate.leave for many elements with the same parent element in a short amount of time, less than 10 ms. In the second sample, the ngClass directive called $animate.addClass for three elements of the same parent element at the same time.

So, if we want to create staggering effects for custom directives, we just have to follow the same rule.

Let's see a sample, check the HTML content with our custom directive, addDirective:

```
<!DOCTYPE html>
<html ng-app="myApp">
<head>
  <title>AngularJS Staggering animations</title>
  <link href="staggered.css" rel="stylesheet" />
</head>
<body>
  <h1>Custom directive Staggering animation</h1>
  <p>Click on above to create elements:</p>
  <div add-directive="">
    <div>Click here!</div>
  </div>
  <script src="//ajax.googleapis.com/ajax/libs/angularjs/1.3.0/
angular.min.js"></script>
  <script src="//ajax.googleapis.com/ajax/libs/angularjs/1.3.0/
angular-animate.min.js"></script>
  <script src="staggeredCtrl.js"></script>
</body>
</html>
```

The following is the custom directive JavaScript in the staggeredCtrl.js file:

```
function addDirectiveFn($animate) {
    return {
      link: function ($scope, $element, $attrs) {
        var firstElement = angular.element('<div
        class="addAnimation">1</div>');
        var secondElement = angular.element('<div
          class="addAnimation">2</div>');
```

```
        var thirdElement = angular.element('<div
          class="addAnimation">3</div>');

          $element.on('click', function () {
            $animate.enter(firstElement, $element);
            $animate.enter(secondElement, $element);
            $animate.enter(thirdElement, $element);

              //Trigger digest in this case, because this listener
function is out of the angular world
            $scope.$apply();
          });
        }
      }
}

angular.module('myApp', ['ngAnimate'])
    .directive('addDirective', addDirectiveFn);
```

The addDirective custom directive just entered three elements on the div element
by clicking on the Click Here text.

The CSS with the stagger class definition is as follows:

```
/* add custom directive animation */
.addAnimation.ng-enter {
    -webkit-transition: opacity ease-in-out 1s;
    transition: opacity ease-in-out 1s;
}

.addAnimation.ng-enter {
    opacity: 0;
}

.addAnimation.ng-enter-stagger {
    -webkit-transition-delay: 0.2s;
    transition-delay: 0.2s;
    -webkit-transition-duration: 0;
    transition-duration: 0;
}

.addAnimation.ng-enter.ng-enter-active {
    opacity: 1;
}
```

This a basic sample of how to create staggering animations on custom directives. This might be useful if you create a custom `ngRepeat` directive and many other cases, as long as we follow the staggering constraints described on the last topic.

At the time of writing this book, there is no trivial way to create staggering animations using JavaScript animations.

You can learn more about staggering animations and a nontrivial workaround to trigger staggering animations using JavaScript at `http://www.yearofmoo.com/2013/12/staggering-animations-in-angularjs.html`.

This is a great blog with a lot of articles about AngularJS animations and samples too.

Summary

In this chapter, we learned how to create staggering animations with AngularJS native and custom directives, so we can now create better animations for web apps.

This feature enables us to accomplish one of the animation guidelines from the material design and the hierarchical timing by creating a motion that supports the information hierarchy. A staggering animation can create a path for the eyes to follow the information being added to the view.

At this point of the book, we might be very excited about how much can be done by so little CSS and JavaScript code with AngularJS. However, we should not forget about the performance of our web app, so the next chapter will focus on how to avoid animation jank and how to find bottlenecks in our web apps.

8

Animations' Performance Optimization

We have already learned how to create different animations using AngularJS, CSS, and JavaScript, but we must always be concerned with the user experience. All animations in separate samples are great, and performance is not an issue. However, when we are dealing with big single-page applications with heavy processing, a lot of CSS and a big DOM, we should focus on keeping our web app fast and the animations smooth; this is the topic of this chapter.

In this chapter, we will learn the following topics:

- Display and the frame rate
- Finding performance bottlenecks using Chrome DevTools
- Measuring browser layers and Jank on Chrome
- CSS styles in animations you should avoid

The display and the frame rate

Each device and monitor display has a regular refresh interval. A usual monitor frequency is 60 Hz, which means that the display will refresh 60 times per second, and a new frame will be displayed approximately every 16 ms.

JavaScript animations can use setInterval or setTimeout using 16 ms (60 frames per second), as this is a commonly used refresh rate. It's not a good idea to use this hardcoded value, as different devices have different refresh rates and the timer precision is not reliable.

We are able to work around this vulnerability using the requestAnimationFrame function. It receives callback functions like the setInterval and setTimeout functions do, but requestAnimationFrame only calls the callback function when the browser is going to produce a new frame before the next repaint.

To support older browsers, some vendor-specific code can be used as well, as described in the following code:

```
window.requestAnimationFrame = window.requestAnimationFrame || window.
mozRequestAnimationFrame || window.webkitRequestAnimationFrame ||
window.msRequestAnimationFrame;
```

Check the next animation sample using requestAnimationframe, based on the animations of *Chapter 1, Getting Started*, which we created using JavaScript and CSS without AngularJS.

The HTML of this sample is as follows:

```
<!DOCTYPE html>
<html>
<head>
    <title>Performance</title>
    <link href="performance.css" rel="stylesheet" />
</head>
<body>
    <h1>Animation with javascript</h1>
    <!--There is a click listener for this button -->
    <button id="jsBtn">Click here to move with JS</button>
    <div id="jsanimation">
        This block will be moved
    </div>
    <script src="performance.js"></script>
</body>
</html>
```

The CSS of the performance.css file is as follows:

```
#jsanimation
{
    position: relative;
}
#cssanimation {
    position:relative;
    -webkit-transition: all 2s ease-in-out;
```

```
        transition: all 2s ease-in-out;
}


.move-to-right {
    -webkit-transform: translate(100px,0);
    transform: translate(100px,0);
}
```

The JavaScript animation that uses the `requestAnimationFrame` function in the `performance.js` file is as follows:

```
window.requestAnimationFrame = window.requestAnimationFrame || window.
mozRequestAnimationFrame || window.webkitRequestAnimationFrame ||
window.msRequestAnimationFrame;

var jsAnimationElement = document.getElementById('jsanimation');
var jsAnimationBtn = document.getElementById('jsBtn');

//This global variable holds the position left of the div
var positionLeft = 0;

function moveToRight() {
    positionLeft += 10;
    /* Set position left of the jsanimation div */
    jsAnimationElement.style.left = positionLeft + 'px';
    if (positionLeft < 100) {
        requestAnimationFrame(moveToRight);
    }
}

jsAnimationBtn.addEventListener('click', function
moveBtnClickListener() {
    requestAnimationFrame(moveToRight);
}, false);
```

This sample uses **Request Animation Frame (RAF)**; so, the callback function that moves the element 10 px will be called before each repaint until the element has moved 100 px to the right. If we set a hardcoded time interval using the `setTimeout` function, we might lose a repaint. Losing repaints gives the user a feeling of lag.

Although RAF helps improve the animation quality, we still have to keep in mind that a new frame is often generated every 16 ms, so the browser has 16 ms to compute the JavaScript, manipulate DOM, execute the layout, paint and anything else, otherwise you will lose a frame and the animation smoothness might be degraded.

There is a great article on the request animation frame and rendering performance at `http://www.html5rocks.com/en/tutorials/speed/rendering/`.

In *Chapter 1, Getting Started*, we talked about browsers that could layer CSS animations and separate rendering from the JavaScript thread and other page layers, like Chrome and Chrome for Android do.

As CSS animations' execution is separated from the JavaScript execution, it's easy to see that modern browsers can improve the animation's smoothness. The animation frame is ready independent of the JavaScript execution. If you execute a heavy loop and it keeps processing in JavaScript, your JavaScript animation might fail (freeze), as the thread will already be busy processing the loop. This is why we should always prefer CSS animations instead of JavaScript animations, in my humble opinion.

In the following topic, we will learn how to find out whether our animations are losing frames.

Finding performance bottlenecks using Chrome DevTools

We just learned the benefits of using `requestFrameRate` and CSS animations. However, if we want to improve our animations' performance, how can we find out what is slowing things down?

Nowadays, we have tools that help us find these bottlenecks, and one of them is Chrome DevTools, which is a collection of tools that comes with the Chrome browser. To open Chrome DevTools, just press *F12* or click on any part of a page, and then click on **Inspect element**. This tool is very familiar for web developers. Now, we will learn how to analyze the timeline frames mode.

We need to record the execution, so Chrome will show us a real-time report with the frame rate, as shown in the following screenshot:

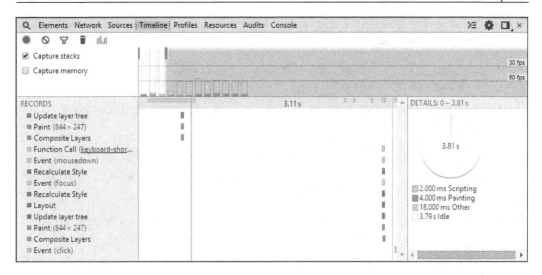

The top-right timeline has lines for 30 fps and 60 fps, and the height of each vertical bar on Frames View represents the time it took to complete a frame and send it to the screen. So, if we have vertical bars above the 60 fps horizontal line or above the 30 fps line, we are skipping frames. We can focus on a specific time range in order to analyze what happened in between.

Usually, a frame is displayed after the JavaScript execution, Style and layout, **Paint**, and **Compositing Layers**. The paint phase is the biggest one, so we should be careful with it; this is a common scrolling bottleneck.

Chrome DevTools separate the steps of a frame and how long each step takes, as shown in the following screenshot:

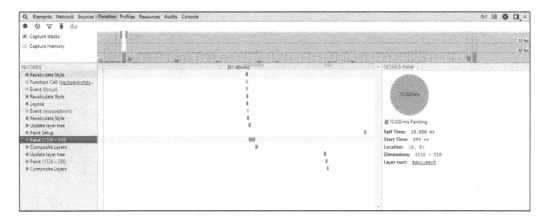

There are some operations that trigger layout, others trigger paint, and a few only trigger composite layers:

- Changing the `width`, `height`, `margin`, `left`, `right`, `top`, and `bottom` position will cause a layout step.

- Applying `box-shadow`, `border-radius`, and `background` will cause a paint step.

- Using `transform` and `opacity` will just cause a layer-compositing phase.

These rules apply for Chrome at the time of writing this book; this might change in the future as browsers are constantly evolving.

There is a reference with full CSS properties and the operations they trigger at `http://csstriggers.com/`.

What we always need to do is use tools in order to find the bottlenecks in our web apps.

Checking FPS using Show fps meter

We can use the *Show fps meter* rendering tool from Chrome DevTools too so that we can check the frames per second as we trigger animations. On Chrome DevTools, open the drawer. The following screenshot shows us the position of the drawer button:

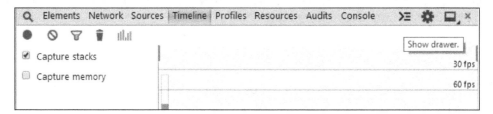

Go to the drawer **Rendering** tab and check **Show FPS meter**, so that an FPS meter will be displayed over the page; we can start triggering animations and check whether any of them is causing a problem.

We can see the **Show FPS meter** option enabled in the following screenshot:

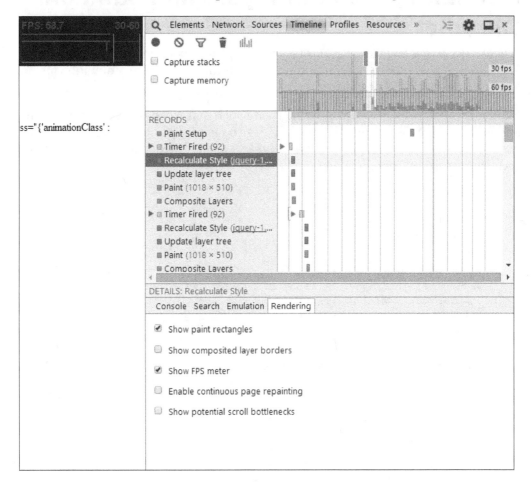

We are able to diagnose Android devices with remote debugging too. Using the remote debugger with Chrome, a timeline on our desktop browser is displayed with the data from the Chrome device in real time.

You can learn more about Chrome's remote debugging setup at
`https://developer.chrome.com/devtools/docs/remote-debugging`.

Measuring browser layers and Jank on Chrome

We just saw that using Chrome DevTools helps us find performance bottlenecks. Now, we are going to see how to find paint layers and enhance an animation just by replacing some CSS properties.

For this sample, we will create a sliding menu such that when we click on a button and it slides from the left menu items, the page content slides to the right too. When we click on the button again, both the menu and page content slides to the left until the menu vanishes from the viewport.

The following HTML will be used:

```html
<!DOCTYPE html>
<html ng-app="myApp">
<head>
  <title>Performance</title>
  <link href="http://ajax.aspnetcdn.com/ajax/bootstrap/3.2.0/css/
bootstrap.css" rel="stylesheet" />
  <link href="performance.css" rel="stylesheet" />
</head>
<body>
  <div id="menu" data-ng-show="showMenu">
    <nav class="navbar-collapse bs-navbar-collapse collapse in">
      <ul class="nav navbar-nav">
        <li><a>menu item 1</a></li>
        <li><a>menu item 2</a></li>
        <li><a>menu item 3</a></li>
        <li><a>menu item 4</a></li>
        <li><a>menu item 5</a></li>
        <li><a>menu item 6</a></li>
        <li><a>menu item 7</a></li>
      </ul>
    </nav>
  </div>
  <div id="content">
    <button ng-click="showMenu = !showMenu">Menu</button>
    <h1>Main content</h1>
    <p>
      Lorem ipsum text Lorem ipsum text Lorem ipsum text Lorem ipsum
text Lorem ipsum text
      Lorem ipsum text Lorem ipsum text Lorem ipsum text Lorem ipsum
text Lorem
```

```
      ipsum text Lorem ipsum text Lorem ipsum text Lorem ipsum text
Lorem ipsum text
  </div>
  <script src="//ajax.googleapis.com/ajax/libs/angularjs/1.3.0/
angular.min.js"></script>
  <script src="//ajax.googleapis.com/ajax/libs/angularjs/1.3.0/
angular-animate.min.js"></script>
  <script>
    angular.module('myApp', ['ngAnimate']);
  </script>
</body>
</html>
```

We will add the slide animation using the CSS transition for the left property, as we can see in the following CSS code:

```
#menu.ng-hide-add {
    transition: transform ease-in-out 0.3s;
    transform: translateX(0px);
}


#menu.ng-hide-add-active {
    transform: translateX(-150px);
}


#menu.ng-hide-remove {
    transition: transform ease-in-out 0.3s;
    transform: translateX(-150px);
}


#menu.ng-hide-remove-active {
    transform: translateX(0px);
}


#menu {
    position: absolute;
    width: 130px;
    background-color: white;
    transform: translateZ(0);
}


#menu.ng-hide + #content {
```

```
        transform: translateX(0px);
    }

    li {
        box-shadow: 1px 1px 1px black;
    }

    #content {
        width: 80%;
        transition: transform ease-in-out 0.3s;
        transform: translateX(150px);
    }
```

Now that we have our sample running, let's check its timeline on Chrome DevTools. This is the initial status before recording:

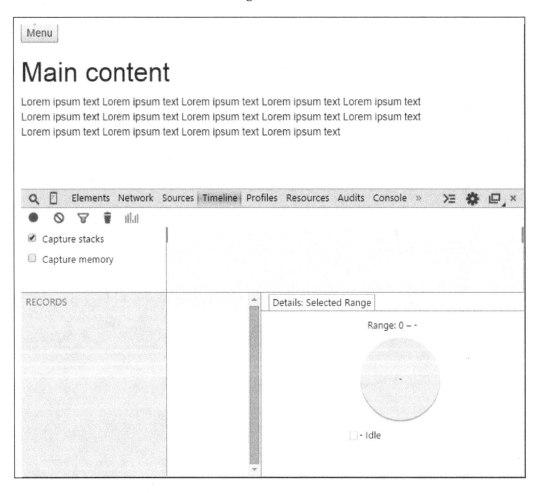

Now, we will click on the **Record** button, and then click on the **Menu** button, wait until the animation has finished, and click again on the **Menu** button and wait until the animation has finished again.

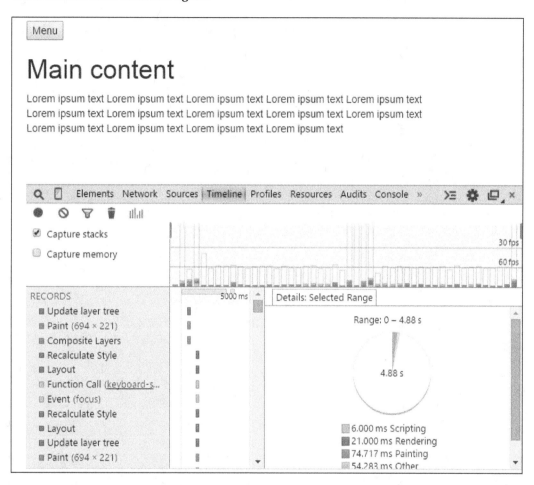

As we can see, we have small peaks of yellow, blue, and purple bars. Yellow means that JavaScript was being processed, blue means that a layout/rendering operation was running, and green means that the painting was happening. For this sample on a desktop, the animation was below the 60 fps line, which sounds good. However, we can see that there are small green bars between the peaks. If we had a web app with more paint expensive properties, these bars would grow and might cause Jank. The real-world cases are worse than what we reproduced in this sample, as many CSS codes might be changing DOM at the same time, increasing the layout, paint, and JavaScript bars.

Just to show a worse case, let's add more content to the main view and text-shadow to all the text. We will check the same steps being reproduced in the timeline, as shown in the following screenshot:

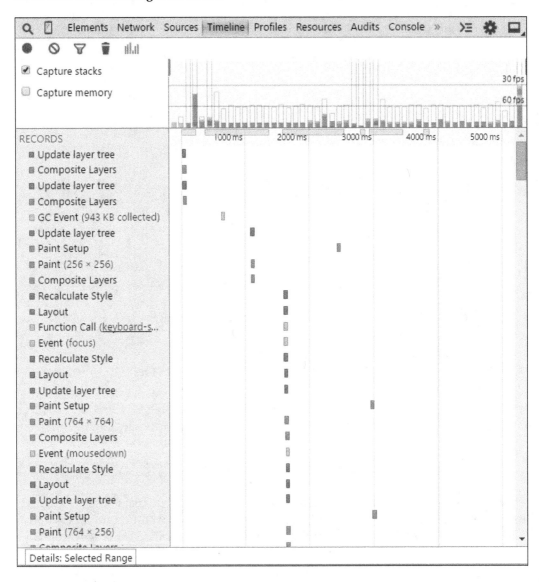

We can see that the paint bars have increased their size, even above the 60 fps line, which is undesirable.

So, we will try to reduce the paint cost by changing the left property animation using the transform:translateX() CSS property to be animated.

So, the same initial situation or sample will have the same HTML. However, a new performance.css file is as follows:

```css
#menu.ng-hide-add {
    transition: transform ease-in-out 0.3s;
    transform: translateX(0px);
}

#menu.ng-hide-add-active {
    transform: translateX(-150px);
}

#menu.ng-hide-remove {
    transition: transform ease-in-out 0.3s;
    transform: translateX(-150px);
}

#menu.ng-hide-remove-active {
    transform: translateX(0px);
}

#menu {
    position: absolute;
    width: 130px;
    background-color: white;
    transform: translateZ(0);
}

#menu.ng-hide + #content {
    transform: translateX(0px);
}

li {
    box-shadow: 1px 1px 1px black;
}

#content {
    width: 80%;
    transition: transform ease-in-out 0.3s;
    transform: translateX(150px);
}
```

We will try again, following the same steps that we used the last time and record the timeline. The result will be as follows:

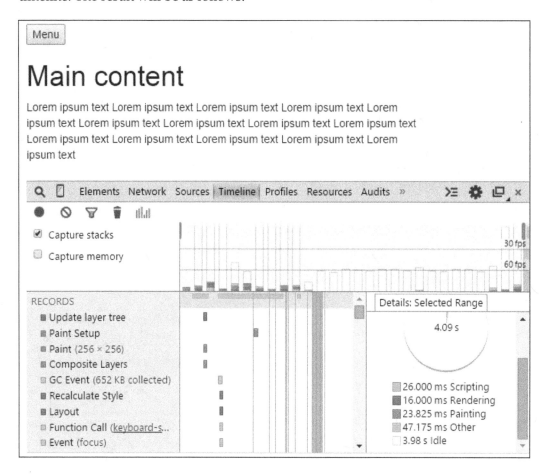

As we can see, the total paint time has been reduced to 23 ms, which is way less than the case in which we used the `left` CSS property animation, which took 74 ms.

Now, let's check the timeline of the same steps but using more content for the main view and `text-shadow`, as we did in the last sample's worse case too. The new timeline performance will be as follows:

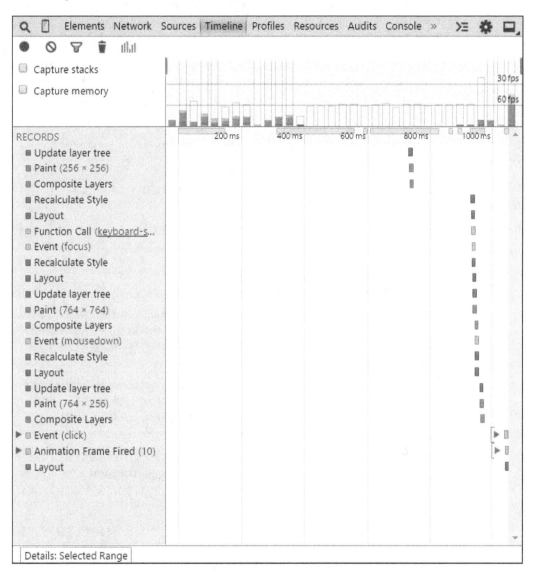

As we can see, there are still some peaks but smaller than the same case using the `left` property and more acceptable. In the time between these peaks, the paint was not required or was much smaller than the last sample.

Alright, but where is the trick? Why does one solution have better results than the other?

We used the `transform` property to animate, so Chrome will create a layer that uses the GPU processor instead of the CPU. Okay, but how can we see whether there is a separated layer or not?

Now, we will use another feature of Chrome DevTools. The **Show paint rectangles** and **Show composited layer borders** options are available at the drawer rendering tab, near the **Show FPS meter** option that we saw in the previous section.

Then, we will follow the same steps that we used to check the timeline. The composited layers will be separated by rectangles and the layers painted will be highlighted as green rectangles too.

We can see that the menu has its own layer rectangle, as shown in the following screenshot:

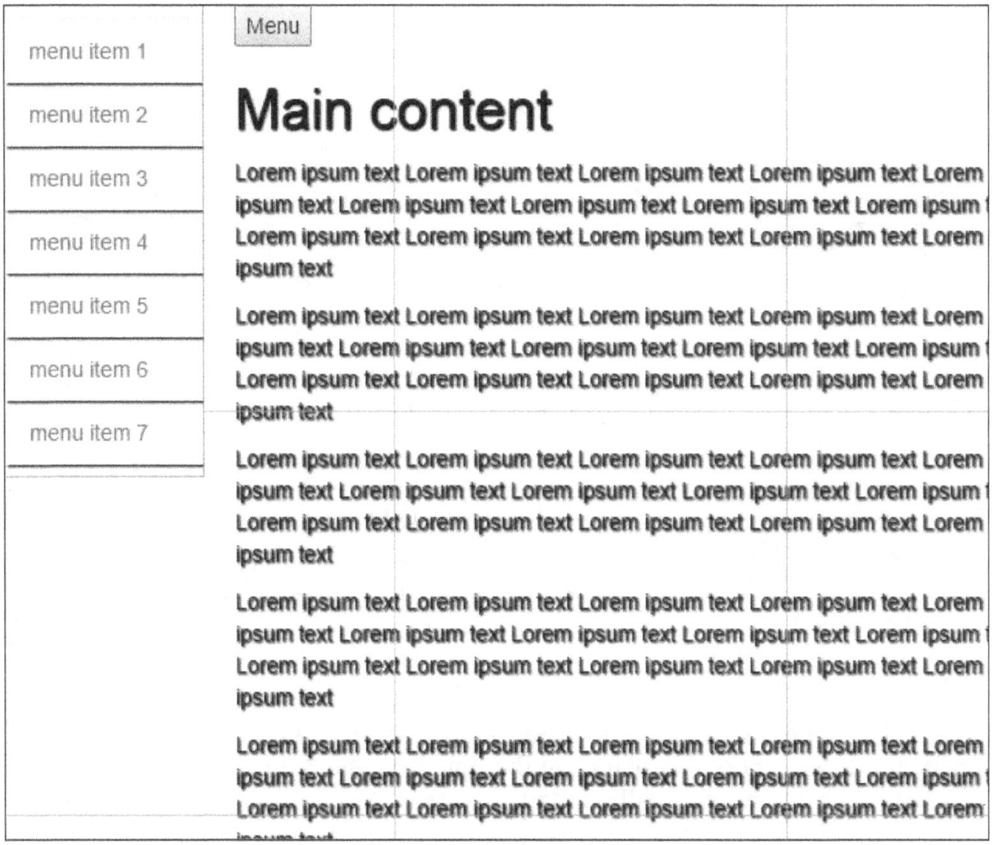

If you are still not convinced, Paul Irish, who is a part of the Google Chrome team, created a video that explains why animations with `transform:translate()` are better than `position:absolute` with `top/left` properties. You can check out the video at `http://www.paulirish.com/2012/why-moving-elements-with-translate-is-better-than-posabs-topleft/`.

CSS styles in animations you should avoid

Position, scale, rotation, and opacity are properties that can be animated without much cost using `transform: translate`, `transform: scale`, `transform: rotate`, and `opacity`. A great tip is to change the `top` and `left` animations using `tranform:translate()` instead, as we did in the last sample. These properties are not frame budget expensive because they only affect composite layers and therefore, they do not need layout and paint steps.

Some styles affect the layout. This means that if you change the width of an element, other elements might be affected, so the browser will have to recalculate all trees a of elements before rendering the next frame. This is expensive, and the time it takes increases with the rise in the number of elements in this tree.

There is an article on high performance animations at `http://www.html5rocks.com/en/tutorials/speed/high-performance-animations/`.

Some styles that affect the layout, apart from many others, are listed in the this order of the most used layouts to the least used: `Width, height, padding, margin, display, border-width, border, top, position, font-size, float, background-color, border-color, text-align, overflow, font-weight, right,` and `bottom`.

The separation of layers helps the performance, because it is assisted by GPU. The layer-creation rules are determined by each browser; browsers that use WebKit and Blink such as Chrome, Opera, and Safari create layers. There are many variables that Chrome uses in order to determine whether it will create a layer; here, I list two important rules:

- The layer has 3D or perspective transform CSS properties.
- The layer uses a CSS animation for its opacity. It uses an animated webkit transform.

So, there is a trick to create layers if we use the following:

```
-webkit-transform: translateZ(0);
transform: translateZ(0);
```

Or, we can use the following:

```
-webkit-transform: translate3d(0,0,0);
transform: translate3d(0,0,0);
```

A new layer will be created for the element and will help in rendering the performance. You should test adding it to an element in order to measure whether FPS was improved upon.

However, if we add too many layers, processing might cause poor performance, because the video memory might be very limited on devices. The overuse of layers processed by the GPU can slow down the page too.

A great article on the layer performance hack can be found at `http://aerotwist.com/blog/on-translate3d-and-layer-creation-hacks/`

We must keep in mind that we can enhance the user experience by creating animations, but if we don't test and analyze each use case, we might have created a rendering bottleneck instead of delivering a best quality app. There is no way to simulate performance on mobile devices using desktops, as each browser has different behaviors and different cores in different platforms.

There is a website that is focused on articles and videos that teach how to avoid, diagnose, and solve the poor performance of websites, including the performance of animations that I recommend for all the readers to check out. The website is `http://jankfree.org/`.

Summary

In this final chapter, we learned how to diagnose animations' performance using Chrome DevTools so that we can create smooth animations for web apps and find out when our animations need to be changed or adjusted.

At this point, we are ready to create the most versatile animations using AngularJS and web standards using different approaches, analyze how to accomplish this, and diagnose whether they're skipping frames. Now, we are able to deliver single-page applications with animations and the best quality user experience after knowing the limitations of modern web browsers and how to measure performance.

Index

Symbols

$animate.addClass method 106
$animate.enter method 107
$animate.leave method 108
$animate methods 104
$animate.move method
  using 111-113
$animate.removeClass method 106

A

AngularJS
  about 7, 47, 49
  animations convention 51, 52
  URL 47, 66
  used, for creating fade animations 49-51
  versions 48
AngularJS 2.0 Touch Animations 128
AngularJS animation
  binding, with CSS keyframe
    animations 58-61
  binding, with CSS transitions 52-54
  creating, without CSS3 83-88
  need for 9, 10
  ng-enter class, using 54
  ngHide JavaScript animation 90
  ngIf JavaScript animation 92
  ng-leave class, using 56
  ngRepeat JavaScript animation 95
AngularJS animations convention 51, 52
animatable properties
  about 28-31
  examples 28
  URL 28

animation-delay property 36
animation-direction property 36
animation-fill-mode property 36
animation-iteration-count property 36
animation-name property 34
animation-play-state property 36
animations
  definition 8
  JavaScript usage, selecting 10-16
  triggering, on custom directives 103-107
  used, for enhancing UX on mobile
    devices 119, 120
authentic motion 120

B

beforeAddClass callback function 90
Bower
  URL 48
browser layers
  measuring, on Chrome 152
  measuring, on Jank 152-161

C

Central Processing Unit (CPU) 10
Chrome
  browser layers, measuring on 152
Chrome DevTools (Chrome Developer
  Tools)
  about 54
  used, for searching performance
    bottlenecks 148, 149
content distribution network (CDN) 47
Cordova
  URL 129

H

high performance animations
URL 11, 161

I

Ionic
URL 129

J

Jank
browser layers, measuring on 152-161
JavaScript
combining, with CSS3 16
JavaScript animations
using, as fallback for CSS
animations 97-100
jQuery
URL 83

K

keyframes
used, for defining animations 32-34

L

leave events
animating 107-110
linear property 25

M

material design
URL 120
Microsoft CDN libraries
URL 66
mobile AngularJS frameworks
Cordova 129
Ionic 129
Mobile Angular UI 129
PhoneGap 129
Mobile Angular UI
URL 129
Model View Whatever (MVW) 9
Modernizr
about 97

URL 97
Modernizr.cssanimations property 100

N

native directives
staggering animations,
creating for 138-140
ngAnimate module
about 9
setup 47, 48
usage 47, 48
ngClass directive animation sample 62-65
ng-enter class 54, 55
ngHide JavaScript animation 90, 91
ngIf JavaScript animation 92-94
ngInclude directive sample 79-81
ng-leave class 56-58
ngMessages directive animation 70-73
ngModel directive 69, 70
ngRepeat directive 62
ngRepeat JavaScript animation 95-97
ngSwitch directive animation 77-79
ngView directive animation
about 74-76
ngInclude directive sample 79
ngSwitch directive animation 77

P

performance bottlenecks
searching, with Chrome DevTools 148, 149
PhoneGap
URL 129
properties, CSS3 keyframe animations
animation-delay 36
animation-direction 36
animation-fill-mode 36
animation-iteration-count 36
animation-play-state 36

R

remote debugging setup, Chrome 151
removeClass callback function 90
Request Animation Frame (RAF)
about 147
URL 148

S

scale function
  about 41, 42
  using 41
Show fps meter
  used, for checking FPS 150, 151
skew function
  about 44
  using 44
skewX() function 44
skewY() function 44
staggering animations
  about 131
  creating 131, 132
  creating, for custom directives 141-143
  creating, for other native directives 138-140
  using, with CSS keyframes
      animation 136, 137
  using, with CSS transition 132-136
Steller animations
  URL 117
step-end property 27
steps(<integer>[,[start | end]]?) property 27
step-start property 27
swipe-to-left gesture animation effect 121

T

timing functions
  separating, for keyframe interval 35
transition-delay property 28
transitioning 120
transition-timing-function property 24
translate function 42, 43
Twitter Bootstrap library
  URL 66

U

UX
  enhancing on mobile devices, with
      animations 119, 120

V

views
  transitioning between 120-128

W

W3C
  URL 8

Thank you for buying
Learning AngularJS Animations

About Packt Publishing

Packt, pronounced 'packed', published its first book "*Mastering phpMyAdmin for Effective MySQL Management*" in April 2004 and subsequently continued to specialize in publishing highly focused books on specific technologies and solutions.

Our books and publications share the experiences of your fellow IT professionals in adapting and customizing today's systems, applications, and frameworks. Our solution based books give you the knowledge and power to customize the software and technologies you're using to get the job done. Packt books are more specific and less general than the IT books you have seen in the past. Our unique business model allows us to bring you more focused information, giving you more of what you need to know, and less of what you don't.

Packt is a modern, yet unique publishing company, which focuses on producing quality, cutting-edge books for communities of developers, administrators, and newbies alike. For more information, please visit our website: www.packtpub.com.

About Packt Open Source

In 2010, Packt launched two new brands, Packt Open Source and Packt Enterprise, in order to continue its focus on specialization. This book is part of the Packt Open Source brand, home to books published on software built around Open Source licenses, and offering information to anybody from advanced developers to budding web designers. The Open Source brand also runs Packt's Open Source Royalty Scheme, by which Packt gives a royalty to each Open Source project about whose software a book is sold.

Writing for Packt

We welcome all inquiries from people who are interested in authoring. Book proposals should be sent to author@packtpub.com. If your book idea is still at an early stage and you would like to discuss it first before writing a formal book proposal, contact us; one of our commissioning editors will get in touch with you.

We're not just looking for published authors; if you have strong technical skills but no writing experience, our experienced editors can help you develop a writing career, or simply get some additional reward for your expertise.

Mastering AngularJS Directives

ISBN: 978-1-78398-158-8   Paperback: 210 pages

Develop, maintain, and test production-ready directives for any AngularJS-based application

1. Explore the options available for creating directives, by reviewing detailed explanations, and real-world examples.

2. Dissect the life cycle of a directive and understand why they are the base of the AngularJS framework.

3. Discover how to create structured, maintainable, and testable directives through a step-by-step, hands-on approach to AngularJS.

Dependency Injection with AngularJS

ISBN: 978-1-78216-656-6   Paperback: 78 pages

Design, control, and manage your dependencies with AngularJS dependency injection

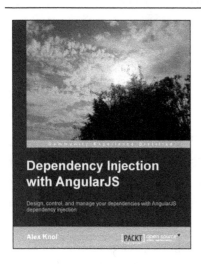

1. Understand the concept of dependency injection.

2. Isolate units of code during testing JavaScript using Jasmine.

3. Create reusable components in AngularJS.

Please check **www.PacktPub.com** for information on our titles

AngularJS Directives

ISBN: 978-1-78328-033-9   Paperback: 110 pages

Learn how to craft dynamic directives to fuel your single-page web applications using AngularJS

1. Learn how to build an AngularJS directive.

2. Create extendable modules for plug-and-play usability.

3. Build apps that react in real time to changes in your data model.

Mastering Web Application Development with AngularJS

ISBN: 978-1-78216-182-0   Paperback: 372 pages

Build single-page web applications using the power of AngularJS

1. Make the most out of AngularJS by understanding the AngularJS philosophy and applying it to real-life development tasks.

2. Effectively structure, write, test, and finally deploy your application.

3. Add security and optimization features to your AngularJS applications.

4. Harness the full power of AngularJS by creating your own directives.

Please check **www.PacktPub.com** for information on our titles

www.ingramcontent.com/pod-product-compliance
Lightning Source LLC
LaVergne TN
LVHW081343050326
832903LV00024B/1279